TROLLOPE AND THE LAW

TROLLOPE AND THE LAW

R. D. McMaster

Professor of English
University of Alberta

St. Martin's Press
New York

First Published in the United States of America in 1986

Printed in Hong Kong

ISBN 0–312–81891–2

Library of Congress Cataloging-in-Publication Data
McMaster, Rowland.
Trollope and the law.
Bibliography: p.
Includes index.
1. Trollope, Anthony, 1815–1882—Knowledge—Law.
2. Trollope, Anthony, 1815–1882—Characters—Lawyers.
3. Law in literature.   4. Lawyers in literature.
I.   Title.
PR5688.L36M34   1986   823'.8   86–1274
ISBN 0–312–81891–2

To Juliet

Contents

Acknowledgements

I record here my gratitude to the people and institutions who have enabled me to write this book: to the Social Sciences and Humanities Research Council of Canada, for a leave fellowship to work on it; to the University of Alberta, for a research grant that enabled me to consult the Trollope papers in the Bodleian; to the Bodleian Library, and to Lloyds Bank, the Trollope Trustees, for permission to quote from those manuscripts; to the National Library of Ireland and to the Biddle Law Library, University of Pennsylvania, for providing me with information from their collections. Chapter 7, © 1981 by the Regents of the University of California, is reprinted from *Nineteenth-Century Fiction*, vol. 36, No. 2, September 1981, pp. 135–156, by permission of the Regents.

My warm personal thanks are due to Professor W. F. Bowker, Director Emeritus of the Institute for Law Research and Reform, at the University of Alberta, a humane and learned friend, who helped me through many a legal and historical problem puzzling to the layman. For kind encouragement, I am grateful to Professors Ruth ap Roberts and John Hall. And most of all my thanks are due to Professor Juliet McMaster, a learned Trollopian, and, most happily for me, my wife.

Texts and Abbreviations

I have used the Oxford World's Classics editions of Trollope's novels with the exception of *The Macdermots of Ballycloran* (London: John Lane, 1906). References are by volume number (in cases where the original issue was two volumes) and page. For other works of Trollope, I have used: *An Autobiography*, World's Classics paperback edition, edited by Michael Sadleir and Frederick Page with introduction and notes by P. D. Edwards (Oxford: Oxford University Press, 1980); *Thackeray* (London, 1879); *The Life of Cicero* (London, 1880); and *The New Zealander*, edited by John Hall (Oxford: Clarendon Press, 1972).

AA	*An Autobiography*	*OF*	*Orley Farm*
CYFH	*Can You Forgive Her?*	*PF*	*Phineas Finn*
ED	*The Eustace Diamonds*	*PR*	*Phineas Redux*
LC	*The Life of Cicero*	*RH*	*Ralph the Heir*
MM	*Miss Mackenzie*	*TC*	*The Three Clerks*
NZ	*The New Zealander*	*WWLN*	*The Way We Live Now*

Preface

Several distinguished scholars have drawn attention to the importance of law and lawyers in Trollope's fiction, and lawyers themselves have taken a steady interest in his works. That more has not been written on the subject is perhaps explained by the apprehensiveness it arouses: a literary critic is apt to be daunted by the technicalities of law, and lawyers may feel that literary criticism is not their line. But then, Trollope himself was not a lawyer, and what we are interested in are those aspects of the law that were of essential importance to him or which clarify the meaning of his works. Such investigation is timely in that the social history of English law is, to judge by recent studies, a matter of increasing general interest. I think I am not merely displaying a partisan interest in the subject when I see the law as having central importance in Trollope's view of society, more important than the Church, the secular life of which he depicts in the Barchester series, and of equal importance with politics, which the law blends with and on which he concentrates in the Palliser series. In the law, Trollope finds not only a machinery for the practical functioning of society but an expression of spiritual principles integral to the English way of doing things. This philosophical view of English law, however, goes along with a good deal of satire, some of it misguided, on the venality and viciousness of lawyers and the harshness of certain legal procedures.

Looking at Trollope's novels in the light of nineteenth-century English legal history has some practical advantages for the interpreting reader. It is over a century since Trollope died. Practices that we take for granted – for instance, that the prisoner in a criminal trial has a right to defence counsel, or that the prisoner can be called as a witness to give sworn testimony, etc. – were either fairly recent or not yet allowed. For the American, Commonwealth, or foreign reader, further mysteries may develop. One American lawyer finds nothing wrong in the action of Trollope's defence counsel, Mr Chaffanbrass, interviewing opposing witnesses before a trial. It would not be wrong – in America. Again, the profession in England is divided into barristers and solicitors, each with their separate functions, rights of court appearance, traditions, class status, and relationships with clients. American or Canadian lawyers combine both functions and call themselves by the double-barrelled signification, 'barrister and solicitor'. An English barrister, however, would be miffed to be called an attorney (as one reference book on Trollope calls Mr Chaffanbrass) – that would mean he was a solicitor, not a barrister, and lower in the social pecking order. Such intricacies and distinctions are the stuff of Trollope's fiction, and to explore their operation is to discover essential aspects of his meaning.

My object, then, has been to explore law and lawyers in Trollope's novels in the light of legal history, traditional attitudes to law, and the philosophy of law. Coral Lansbury, in *The Reasonable Man: Trollope's Legal Fiction* (1981), examined the Trollope canon by applying general techniques of legal pleading which she saw him inheriting indirectly through his Post Office work and turning to use in the argumentative structures of his novels even when they had little overt concern with litigation. Her approach is more embracing but also more metaphorical. I have concerned myself more directly with legal history, with the lives, status and relationship of barristers and solicitors, with institutions like the Old Bailey, the ethics of advocacy, the careers of lawyer-politicians, the land law, the law of election, and jurisprudence. My concern has not been to catalogue all the lawyers (around a hundred) or legal problems in the novels, nor to discuss all the novels, but to illuminate the sorts of legal topics I have just described in those novels which seem most fruitful for the purpose. I hope by these means to contribute something to the critical appreciation of these novels and to knowledge of Trollope's basic ideology as it touches on English society and the way it works.

'And then those terrible meshes of the Law! How is a fictionist, in these excited days, to create the needed biting interest without legal difficulties . . .'

Trollope, *Phineas Finn*, I, Chapter xxix

1   Trollope and the Law: A Prospect

Trollope was the son of a Chancery lawyer and the father of a paper barrister. The plots of his novels repeatedly turn on points of law. And his characters include about a hundred lawyers of various sorts: solicitors, barristers, Chancery lawyers, Old Bailey lawyers, Solicitors and Attorneys General, and numerous judges. They deal with murderers, they handle great estates, and they advise the Crown. Some are raffish bullies, some suave politicians, others reclusive scholars. At the beginning of his career, though he took a confident stance in castigating the failings of lawyers, Trollope was often wrong in his presentation of legal scenes and issues. The reviewers, especially of *Orley Farm*, gave him a drubbing for his inaccuracies, and as he became more concerned to get things right, and as his fame brought him into the company of distinguished lawyers and judges, he occasionally sought legal advice to see that his facts were straight and his terms correct when he concocted litigations of unusual complexity. He had not just the average novelists's need to deal on occasion with the legal consequences of marriage, death or inheritance but a keen interest in the intricacies of law as expressing and sustaining social order and accommodation, as spinning between individuals, families and generations the cobweb of finely adjusted interests that constitutes the English way of life.

Trollope's father, Thomas Anthony Trollope, had the scholarship and industry to succeed in legal practice, but not the personality. A graduate of Winchester School and Fellow of New College, Oxford, Thomas, says Trollope's biographer, Michael Sadleir,

> was unremitting in his application to a profession not ultimately vital to his livelihood [he expected an inheritance

1

that ultimately failed to come his way]. He impressed his
seniors and his colleagues by his knowledge and understanding of law and was regarded as among the most
learned of the junior Chancery barristers. But more than
learning is required to build and to maintain a legal
practice. . . . He had the intellect and the application necessary to achievement, but of the even more necessary humil-
ity, elasticity and readiness to see another point of view, he
had none at all. He was dour and unapproachable, sullen
under occasional defeat, arrogant in victory. . . . Trollope
offended his colleagues and, worse still, his clients.[1]

A barrister, in the English system, depends for employment
on attorneys, who seek him out with briefs for specific cases,
but his father, says Trollope in *An Autobiography*, was 'plagued
with so bad a temper, that he drove the attorneys from
him'(3).

Thomas kept 'dingy, almost suicidal chambers, at No. 23
Old Square, Lincoln's Inn, – chambers which on one melan-
choly occasion did become absolutely suicidal' when one of his
students killed himself there (2–3). Among Anthony's recol-
lections of being the family's ugly duckling when a schoolboy
were those of a whole vacation spent cooling his heels in these
gloomy haunts.

> I remember to have passed one set of holidays – the mid-
> summer holidays – in my father's chambers in Lincoln's
> Inn. There was often a difficulty about the holidays, – as to
> what should be done with me. On this occasion my amuse-
> ment consisted in wandering about among those old
> deserted buildings, and in reading Shakespeare out of a bi-
> columned edition which is still among my books. It was not
> that I had chosen Shakespeare, but that there was nothing
> else.   (8–9)

The atmosphere was not lost on him – as we shall see. When
Phineas Finn is trying to choose between Parliament or legal
practice, the thought of 'dingy' chambers in the same Square
helps to dissuade him from the law. The notion of living in a
set of chambers is elaborated in *Ralph the Heir*, where Sir
Thomas Underwood, a Chancery barrister who had become

Solicitor-General briefly, prefers his chambers to the pleasant villa in Fulham where his daughters are largely left to fend for themselves, though he will not admit, or allow them to assert, that he does not live with them.

> He had, indeed, all but abandoned his practice at the Bar, never putting himself forward for the ordinary business of a Chancery barrister. But, nevertheless, he spent the largest half of his life in his chambers, breakfasting there, reading there, writing there, and sleeping there.   (I, 6)

> Sir Thomas's chambers in Southampton Buildings, though they were dull and dingy of aspect from the outside, and were reached by a staircase which may be designated as lugubrious, – so much did its dark and dismantled condition tend to melancholy, – were in themselves large and commodious. His bedroom was small, but he had two spacious sitting rooms, one of which was fitted up as a library, and the other as a dining-room. Over and beyond these there was a clerk's room; for Sir Thomas, though he had given up the greater part of his business, had not given up his clerk; and here the old man, the clerk, passed his entire time, from half-past eight in the morning till ten at night, waiting upon his employer in various capacities with a sedulous personal attention to which he had probably not intended to devote himself when he first took upon himself the duties of clerk to a practising Chancery barrister.   (I, 7)

At night Sir Thomas 'would prowl about the purlieus of Chancery Lane, the Temple, and Lincoln's Inn, till two or even three o'clock in the morning' (I, 11–12). He justifies his seclusion from family and business by dedication to writing a life of Bacon, a work of hopeless erudition like Thomas Trollope's *Encyclopaedia Ecclesiastica*, except that at sixty Sir Thomas has not written a line. At the end of the novel, however, his remaining unmarried daughter persuades him to leave 'those stuffy, dark, dingy, lawyers' chambers' and dwell at home with her (II, 352). The sights and smells of London's legal districts, which Trollope had experienced so gloomily as a child, return again and again in his novels.

From the age of nineteen much of Trollope's life was spent

working in the Post Office. Coral Lansbury bases her study of
Trollope's 'legal fictions' on that experience. When Trollope
was hired, Sir Francis Freeling was Secretary to the Post
Office. Among the many reforms he effected was a change in
the manner of writing of all its letters, reports and minutes.
'Being in control of the Post Office, he had the opportunity to
impose both style and method upon his subordinates, who
learned to write like Freeling or found another occupation.'[2]
The model he chose for such writing was a legal declaration
such as that described in John Frederick Archbold's *A Digest of
the Law Relative to Pleading and Evidence in Actions Real Personal
and Mixed* (London, 1821). The declaration's shape consists of
a commencement, statement of the cause of action, and a
conclusion. The style is to be plain, simple, clear and factual.
Lansbury's contention is that Trollope absorbed this technique thoroughly: 'Official writing was to influence the structure of his novels just as legal modes of examination and
evidence came to define his narrative art.'[3] Observing 'It has
always been overlooked that Trollope wrote as much for the
Post Office as he did for his reading public,'[4] she sees the way
of thinking and writing he so acquired as affecting not only
the manner of his prose style and plot development but the
characteristic way he develops his fictions as though a case
were being considered subtly in all its dimensions and a
judgement gradually encouraged in the reader.

The Post Office could be said to have brought Trollope into
close consideration of the law in another way by sending him
to Ireland as a surveyor's clerk in 1841. 'I was at that time in
dire trouble, having debts on my head and quarrels with our
Secretary-Colonel, and a full conviction that my life was
taking me downwards to the lowest pits. So I went to the
Colonel boldly, and volunteered for Ireland if he would send
me. He was glad to be so rid of me and I went' (*AA*, 58). From
that time, Trollope's life became happy and successful. His
efforts to impose efficiency and honesty in the postal service
were carried out with a mixture of bullying panache and
detective cunning, and on occasion, as we shall see in a later
chapter, took him into the courts as a prosecution witness.
And what he saw was grist for his mill from the first. His early
novels contain several Irish courtroom scenes. It has been
argued, with what justice it is difficult to determine, that the

Irish Bar was even more ferocious than the English Bar, whose methods of cross-examination Trollope deplored throughout his life.[5] Moreover, the Irish enjoyed a reputation for litigiousness as one of the principle pleasures of life. Maria Edgeworth, in notes for her novel *Castle Rackrent* (1800), one of the first regional novels in English and about Ireland, describes this Irish enthusiasm:

almost every poor man in Ireland, be he farmer, weaver, shopkeeper, or steward, is, beside his other occupations, occasionally a lawyer. The nature of processes, ejectments, custodians, injunctions, replevins, &c. &c. are perfectly known to them, and the terms are as familiar to them as to any attorney. They all love law. It is a kind of lottery, in which every man, staking his own wit or cunning against his richer neighbour's property, feels that he has little to lose and much to gain.

'I'll have the law of you, so I will!' – is the saying of an Englishman who expects justice. 'I'll have you before his honor' – is the threat of an Irishman who hopes for partiality. Miserable is the life of a justice of the peace in Ireland the day after a fair, especially if he resides near a small town. The multitude of the *kilt* (*kilt* does not mean *killed*, but hurt) and wounded who come before his honor with black eyes or bloody heads is astonishing, but more astonishing is the number of those, who, though they are scarcely able by daily labour to procure daily food, will nevertheless, without the least reluctance, waste six or seven hours of the day lounging in the yard or hall of a justice of the peace, waiting to make some complaint about – nothing. It is impossible to convince them that *time is money*. They do not set any value upon their own time, and they think that others estimate theirs at less than nothing. Hence they make no scruple of telling a justice of the peace a story of an hour long about a *tester* (sixpence): and if he grow impatient, they attribute it to some secret prejudice which he entertains against them.

Edgeworth then gives some examples of such stories told '*out of the face*, that is, from the beginning to the end, without interruption', and concluding, 'I'll leave it all to your honor.'

I'll leave *it* all to your honor – literally means, I'll leave all the trouble to your honor.

The Editor knew a justice of the peace in Ireland, who had such a dread of *having it all left to his honor*, that he frequently gave the complainants the sum about which they were disputing to make peace between them, and to get rid of the trouble of hearing their stories *out of the face*. But he was soon cured of this method of buying off disputes, by the increasing multitude of those who, out of pure regard to his honor, came 'to get justice from him, because they would sooner come before him than before any man in all Ireland'.[6]

A century later some of the same conditions and atmosphere are captured by Somerville and Ross in *Some Experiences of an Irish R.M.* (1899). Both Edgeworth and Somerville and Ross present, on the whole, an indulgent view of Irish litigiousness. Trollope, in *The Macdermots of Ballycloran*, explores darker, more murderous animosities, and its courtroom scenes reflect his satirical view of advocates. He gives them names such as O'Blather and Allwinde.

Throughout his life he took a hostile view of advocacy. As a reviewer of *Orley Farm* observed: 'There is . . . one subject which Mr. Trollope pursues with unremitting zeal. He cannot bear a lawyer. They are all rogues, not by nature, but by profession.'[7] There are, indeed, decent and admirable lawyers among the many Trollope created, scholars like Mr Dove, devoted defenders of estates, like Mr Camperdown and Mr Grey, even an imaginative and humane Solicitor-General, Sir William Patterson. Among solicitors, there are decent firms like Slow and Bideawhile, and Trollope even comes to a grudging respect for his savage barrister and denizen of the Old Bailey, Mr Chaffanbrass. But in general, his attitude to lawyers is hostile and satirical. He was a vehement man himself, holding many stiff-necked opinions. As many scholars have observed, however, his novels are singular for the degree to which they sympathetically present all sides of an issue, even the ones that Trollope, as a man, thoroughly disagrees with, such as the feminist views of some of his characters like Lady Glencora or Mrs Hurtle. The central virtue to which virtually all of his novels and estimates of character recur is

truth-telling, but he could be evasive himself.[8] Perhaps these
personal traits account for the great interest he takes in
lawyers and the exasperation with which he represents barristers in particular. His central accusation is that, as a matter of
professional method, they are an untruthful lot. They defend
villains, even when they are pretty sure that the defendant *is* a
villain. They adopt a line in alliance with their client, and
heaping scorn on opposing arguments, present their own
one-sided argument with partisan zeal, badgering and
belittling witnesses and making them feel like fools if not
worse. Imaginatively, nevertheless, in the creation of, and
inner communing with, character in his novels, Trollope was
eventually able, in his characteristic way, to see other sides to
the barrister's character and profession. We shall look at these
matters closely in connection with one of his most vivid creations, Mr Chaffanbrass. But a word may be appropriate here
on the traditional background he was drawing on for his
hostile views, the matrix, as it were, of his prejudices. The
venality of lawyers, their readiness to argue in a bad cause, has
always offended the righteous. God puts down Job for adopting a forensic style. Protagoras and the sophists, arguing the
relativity of truth, and teaching rhetorical skills 'to make the
worse appear the better cause', earned the distrust of Plato
and Aristotle and became a natural object of suspicion and
satire. Their tradition, however, blends with that of the advocate, who, like Cicero, learns their skills and applies them in
the service of clients. English literature is full of satire at the
expense of advocates and their hoodwinking rhetoric:

> Men of your large profession, that could speak
> To every cause, and things mere contraries,
> Till they were hoarse again, yet all be law;
> That, with most quick agility, could turn,
> And re-turn; make knots, and undo them;
> Give forked counsel; take provoking gold
> On either hand, and put it up, . . .

as Jonson says in *Volpone* (I, i, 271–7). Gulliver tells the
Houyhnhnms, 'there was a society of men among us, bred up
from their youth in the art of proving by words multiplied for
the purpose, that white is black, and black is white, according

as they are paid.'[9] The caricature is highly stylised and of long standing. Even lawyers themselves resort to it occasionally. In one of his finest essays, on 'Francis Bacon', Macaulay, who was himself a barrister on the northern circuit, indulges himself in the following *occupatio*:

> We will not at present inquire whether the doctrine which is held on this subject [the advocate's moral discretion in acting for a client of doubtful virtue] by English lawyers be or be not agreeable to reason and morality; whether it be right that a man should, with a wig on his head, and a band round his neck, do for a guinea what, without those appendages, he would think it wicked and infamous to do for an empire; whether it be right that, not merely believing but knowing a statement to be true, he should do all that can be done by sophistry, by rhetoric, by solemn asseveration, by indignant exclamation, by gesture, by play of features, by terrifying one honest witness, by perplexing another, to cause a jury to think that statement false.[10]

The general view of barristers implied in Macaulay's words here is just the one Trollope presents repeatedly in his early novels, particularly, as we shall see, in *Orley Farm*.

With a satirical tradition of such long standing, there are, of course, many distinguished replies on the ethics of advocacy. I shall not attempt to rehearse them, but go to the nub of the matter, which Trollope either misunderstood or refused to accept. Irritation with advocates for arguing vigorously on behalf of unsavoury clients stems from a confusion of the roles of advocate and judge. The most famous statement of the principle, a text frequently quoted by lawyers writing on the subject, is by Dr Johnson:

> Sir William Forbes said, he thought an honest lawyer should never undertake a cause which he was satisfied was not a just one. 'Sir, (said Mr. Johnson) a lawyer has no business with the justice or injustice of the cause which he undertakes, unless his client asks his opinion, and then he is bound to give it honestly. The justice or injustice of the cause is to be decided by the judge. Consider, Sir; what is the purpose of courts of justice? it is, that every man may have

his cause fairly tried, by men appointed to try causes. A lawyer is not to tell what he knows to be a lie: he is not to produce what he knows to be a false deed; but he is not to usurp the province of the jury and of the judge, and determine what shall be the effect of evidence, – what shall be the result of legal argument. As it rarely happens that a man is fit to plead his own cause, lawyers are a class of the community, who, by study and experience, have acquired the art and power of arranging evidence, and of applying to the points at issue what the law has settled. A lawyer is to do for his client all that his client might fairly do for himself, if he could. If, by a superiority of attention, of knowledge, of skill, and a better method of communication, he has the advantage of his adversary, it is an advantage to which he is entitled. There must always be some advantage, on one side or other; and it is better that advantage should be had by talents, than by chance. If lawyers were to undertake no causes till they were sure they were just, a man might be precluded altogether from a trial of his claim, though, were it judicially examined, it might be found a very just claim.'[11]

Thomas Erskine made the same point in a famous part of his defence of Thomas Paine.[12]

The eminent Victorian barrister, judge and man of letters, Sir James Fitzjames Stephen, in an article called 'The Morality of Advocacy' (*Cornhill Magazine*, April 1865), wrote that 'It is, perhaps, however, amongst the lighter class of writers that lawyers of all sorts, and more particularly barristers, are most hardly dealt with.'[13] He goes over the reasons why people may dislike barristers and admits that 'a certain number of ruffians as brutal and false as any of their clients' do exist, 'ignorant of the law and destitute of education', and owing their success to a natural turn for public speaking.[14] These, however, are exceptions who gain a certain notoriety from the more sensational cases reported in the newspapers. He concludes that

It is only in novels that people engage in lawsuits with the conviction that they are in the wrong. In real life there is nothing of which they are more firmly convinced than that they are right, and that if the truth came out it would secure their triumph. . . . The notion that disregard to truth is an

advantage to a barrister, is of all the spiteful commonplaces
which people take a foolish pleasure in repeating upon the
subject, the most absurd.[15]

In all likelihood Trollope read Stephen's article since it
appeared in the same issue of the *Cornhill Magazine* as the last
instalment of *Framley Parsonage*, but, if he did, it made no
convincing impression on him, because his next work, *Orley
Farm*, as we shall see, was so persistently harsh on the decency
and truthfulness of lawyers that it drew hostility from a
number of reviewers for its treatment of the law and lawyers.

We can see two influences about this time having a somewhat softening effect on Trollope's view of law and lawyers, at
least in the direction of acquiring more informed views. The
first, of course, is the critical reaction to inaccuracies and
prejudices in *Orley Farm*; the second, the distinguished
lawyers he met when his social world expanded consequent
upon his election to the Garrick Club and the Athenaeum in
the sixties. These included Sir Henry James, Baron James of
Hereford (1828–1911), himself an excellent criminal
advocate, Solicitor-General briefly (1873), Attorney-General
(1873 and 1880–5), and statesman. He stood for election at
Taunton the same year as Trollope stood at Beverley. Trollope often visited Sir Henry's estate. Another lawyer of great
assistance to Trollope was Charles George Merewether, QC
(1823–84), recorder of Leicester, who also stood for election
unsuccessfully in 1868 at Northampton though he succeeded
later (1874–80). He helped Trollope with the legal opinion
on heirlooms for *The Eustace Diamonds* and also, it seems, with
legal intricacies in *Lady Anna*. A more distinguished lawyer
still was Sir Alexander Cockburn (1802–80), Solicitor and
Attorney-General (1851–6), prosecutor in the famous trial of
William Palmer the Rugeley poisoner (in accordance with the
tradition that the Attorney-General leads the prosecution of
poisoners), Chief Justice of the Common Pleas (1856), and
Lord Chief Justice of England (1859). He had become notable
in defending Palmerston's foreign policy in 1850, and he
helped Trollope in the writing of Trollope's *Lord Palmerston*.
All three had considerable experience at one time or another
of a subject that was to touch Trollope closely, corruption in
elections. Cockburn as a youthful lawyer had considerable

practice in election petitions. Sir Henry gained his seat in 1869 as the result of an election petition and later, in the eighties, drafted and carried a corrupt practices bill. Merewether became a member of a commission to inquire into corrupt practices in 1880. From 1865, when the *Pall Mall Gazette* was founded, Trollope had the opportunity of meeting at the *Pall Mall* dinners James Fitzjames Stephen, who combined a distinguished career in law with that of a man of letters. All of these distinguished lawyers were close acquaintances of Trollope's, generally helpful to him in his knowledge of political and legal affairs, and sometimes directly helpful on points of detail in his writing.

It remains to consider Trollope's work briefly in relation to the evolving law and practice of law in the nineteenth century. As everyone knows, law, like many other areas of activity, underwent profound reforms. The six-hour speech to Parliament on law reform in 1828 by Lord Brougham, 'the legal Hercules of the time', as Trollope calls him (*NZ*, 54), set off a series of commissions that resulted in the overhauling of the laws, legal procedures, and the organisation of the courts. As well as reforming inherited structures, Victorians were busy creating a spate of new statutes to deal with their new industrial and increasingly democratic society. We would not expect Trollope to take a uniform interest in these matters; some interested him keenly, others left him cold. The early Victorian novelists, Dickens, Kingsley, Disraeli, Mrs Gaskell dramatised life in an industrial environment, describing working conditions, sanitation problems and the like. Trollope hardly touches these matters; his world is much more that of country estates and the environment of the professional and upper classes. And what he neglects in modern law is often as significant as what he is up-to-the-minute with.

For convenience, let us look briefly at his work in relation to land law, criminal law, the law of elections, the law relating to women, and at his depiction of the etiquette of relationships between barristers and solicitors, the branches of the English divided profession.

Like Burke, Trollope has a reverential curiosity about the living organism of English life. The law is a sort of skeleton underlying it, giving it shape, allowing for possibilities of action and setting limitations. To the eye of the trained

anatomist, like Blackstone, the skeleton also has an evolutionary history connected to the whole environment of social,
religious, and philosophical attitudes and accomplishments.
What we have seen so far may not have suggested much
reverence in Trollope for anything related to the law. But
when the question is estates, land, inheritance, continuity and
tradition, deeper chords are struck in Trollope's imagination
of society. The area of law most at issue here is land law, and it
is interesting to see how the impression Trollope gives of land
and inheritance matches up against the main traditions of
English law on the subject. Again, we shall look at the matter
in some detail in the chapter on solicitors and estates. Here, I
shall take a general and historical view.

The possession and inheritance of estates is a major subject
in Trollope's works. As in Jane Austen, the attitude one takes
to an estate reveals a great deal about one's character and
general fitness to hold a place in society. The vulgar social-
climber, Melmotte, in *The Way We Live Now*, hopes to gain
status and respectability by buying a country estate. Roger
Carbury, in the same novel, lives in a symbolically moated
mansion, a social conservative, upholding the old traditions of
familial and communal relationship that are disappearing in
the new commercial age represented by Melmotte. In *Ralph
the Heir*, a father pines under a life interest in the estate,
reluctant to improve it for the sake of a feckless heir and
wanting to give it to his illegitimate but admirable son. In *Lady
Anna* a perverse and lecherous aristocrat reveals the extent of
his depravity not only by his sexual skullduggery but by
reducing his real estate to the minimum and accumulating
money instead. UnEnglish. The heir in tail thus gets some
meagre land but, except for the grace of his cousin, no funds
to sustain the appropriate style of an English earl.

What is, perhaps, distinctive in the numerous significant
examples of inheriting land in Trollope is that the two most
frequent modes are by fee tail and by testament; that is, the
owner either owns the property outright and can leave it to
whom he pleases by making a will, or the estate descends by
strict principles of male primogeniture as bound by the entail.
Moreover, even when the owner is free to dispose of his
property as it suits him, he will, on occasion, behave as though
the estate were entailed and leave it to the next male in line.

Roger Carbury justifiably detests his second cousin, Felix, but is gloomily intent on leaving his beloved estate to the cad. That would preserve the English way. Similarly in *Ralph the Heir*, it seems fitter that the estate should go to the feckless heir than that it should go to the illegitimate son who can be trusted to devote himself to the estate and its tenants. But, in fact, the uncomplicated model of entail was not in itself the English way so much as all that.

Two tendencies may be seen at work in the handing down of real property: a conservative tendency stemming from the original owner's determination to keep the property intact and in the family; and a liberal tendency stemming from the heir's feeling that he ought to be able to do what he likes with what he possesses. The fee tail limiting possession to a person and the heirs *of his body*, and restricting inheritance to his lineal descendants, was established by the statute *De Donis Conditionalibus* in 1285. It suited the large landowners, who were also strong in Parliament, but hampered heirs even in exercising ordinary powers of management. 'As the nobility', says Blackstone, 'were always fond of this statute, because it preserved their family estates from forfeiture, there was little hope of procuring a repeal by the legislature' – a gloomy outlook for the elder sons of elder sons. However, sons and lawyers rose to the occasion, setting their wits against *De Donis*; 'by connivance of an active and politic prince, a method was devised to evade it.'[16]

The two devices contrived in the fifteenth century to evade *De Donis* and bar entails were the common recovery and the fine, notable for their extraordinary legal sleight-of-hand and involving fictions of the sort that inspired Bentham to fine vituperation.[17] Nevertheless, they were commonplace. The Fines and Recoveries Act of 1833 abolished them and substituted a simple method of barring entails. Thus, though a reader of Trollope might suspect that a watchful Providence militates against such irreverent practices, there is no inherent difficulty in getting rid of an entail as, in *The Belton Estate*, Will Belton wishes to do in favour of Clara Amedroz when he inherits the Belton Estate upon the death of her father, the previous tenant, an event which leaves her in penury. His advisors, imbued with a sense of the right order of things, attempt to dissuade him, and he eventually marries her, thus

solving the problem. The mystique of pedigree, however, is
provided:

> There is much in the glory of ownership, – of the ownership
> of land and houses, of beeves and woolly flocks, of wide
> fields and thick-growing woods, even when that ownership
> is of late date, when it conveys to the owner nothing but the
> realization of a property on the soil; but there is much more
> in it when it contains the memories of old years; when the
> glory is the glory of race as well as the glory of power and
> property. There had been Beltons of Belton living there for
> many centuries, and now he was the Belton of the day,
> standing on his own ground, – the descendent and repre-
> sentative of the Beltons of old, – Belton of Belton without a
> flaw in his pedigree.   (412)

In the entailed descent of land from generation to generation, another common feature of which Trollope gives
curiously little impression is the 'strict settlement'. Megarry
and Wade explain:

> What often happened was that the son, when he came of
> age, felt the need of ready money and wished to bar the
> entail and sell or mortgage his estate in remainder. But his
> father, instead of consenting to this, would agree to give
> him some immediate share (perhaps an annual income) in
> the property if he would join in a resettlement. Father and
> son would then in collaboration bar the entail, but resettle
> the property, subject to any outstanding jointure and to the
> son's annuity, upon the father for life, remainder to the son
> for life, remainder to the son's eldest son in tail. The land
> was thus tied up for another generation.[18]

And so on, from generation to generation. Strict settlements
date from before the Restoration and could be said to be a
common way of passing on land in England, of some antiquity
and preserving the principle of primogeniture. It is odd that
Trollope should forego the opportunity strict settlements
provide for dramatising the conflict between generations.
The bargaining between father and son would be a rich field
both for painful differences in point of view and for comedy

of the sort Trollope delights us with in *The Way We Live Now*, where old Longestaffe and the eminently respectable firm of Slow and Bideawhile are lined up against young Dolly Longestaffe and his solicitor, the crafty and unrespectable Squercum. I imagine that the dominance of ordinary entails and primogeniture in Trollope's novels goes along with his reverence for a settled social order embodied in their conservative and traditional features.

Primogeniture is an almost holy feature of Trollope's male-dominated world. There was, of course, a clear linkage between the law of primogeniture, the landed economy, and the political power of a landed aristocracy. The connections are concisely and approvingly stated in the first report of the commissioners on the law of real property (1829), even though, as Holdsworth points out, the chairman was an enthusiastic Whig and many who gave evidence were influenced by Bentham:

> Where no disposition is made by will, the whole landed estate descends to the son or other heir male. This, which is called the Law of Primogeniture, appears far better adapted to the constitution and habits of this kingdom than the opposite Law of Equal Partibility, which in a few generations, would break down the aristocracy of the country; and, by the endless subdivision of the soil, must ultimately be unfavourable to agriculture, and injurious to the best interests of the State.[19]

Even in the 1860s, and in the House of Commons rather than the House of Lords, Bagehot observed that 'in number the landed gentry in the House far surpass any other class' and would be despotic if their excessive provinciality did not make them stupid.[20] Despite various attacks and schemes for revising land law in the period, its general features prevailed until 1925. In a 1905 paper on 'The Paradox of the Land Law', Dicey said: 'The paradox of the modern English land law may be thus summed up; the constitution of England has, whilst preserving monarchical forms, become a democracy, but the land law of England remains the land law appropriate to an aristocratic state.'[21] Trollope is thoroughly aware of the oddities and paradoxes of the system he presents with evident

sympathy. In *The American Senator*, a novel in which he amusingly examines the eccentricities of English behaviour and
institutions through the intent critical eye of a rationalistic
American politician, the Senator at last gives a couple of
lectures on the conclusions to which he has come.

> 'Proceeding from hereditary legislature I come to heredi-
> tary property. It is natural that a man should wish to give to
> his children after his death the property which he has
> enjoyed during their life. But let me ask any man here who
> has not been born an eldest son himself, whether it is
> natural that he should wish to give it all to one son. Would
> any man think of doing so, by the light of his own reason, –
> out of his own head as we say? Would any man be so unjust
> to those who are equal in his love, were he not constrained
> by law, and by custom more iron-handed even than the
> law?' The Senator had here made a mistake very common
> with Americans, and a great many voices were on him at
> once. 'What law?' 'There is no law.' 'You know nothing
> about it.' 'Go back and learn.'
>   . . . Then an eager Briton on the platform got up and
> whispered to the Senator for a few minutes, during which
> the murmuring was continued. 'My friend reminds me,'
> said the Senator, 'that the matter is one of custom rather
> than law; and I am obliged to him. But the custom which is
> damnable and cruel, is backed by law which is equally so. If I
> have land I can not only give it all to my eldest son, but I can
> assure the right of primogeniture to his son, though he be
> not yet born. No one I think will deny that there must be a
> special law to enable me to commit an injustice so unnatural
> as that.
>   'Hence it comes that you still suffer under an aristocracy
> almost as dominant, and in its essence as irrational, as that
> which created feudalism.'   (539–40)

Eventually the lecture approaches a state of riot and is sus-
pended, the Senator declaring to himself as he retires 'that the
want of reason among Britishers was so great, that no one
ought to treat them as wholly responsible beings' (545).
    Trollope's superb ability to fuse all these interests in a
moving portrayal of family animosities, traditional English

values, love of the land and frustration in managing it, is demonstrated in *Ralph the Heir*. Here we see an entail being used as an effective means of punishment. Old Newton, offended that his elder son, Gregory, has an illegitimate son, and determined that the property shall descend in the 'true line of the Newtons' (I, 116), urges his younger son, the Parson of Peele Newton, to marry, and makes a settlement of the estate:

> The settlement was natural enough. It simply entailed the property on the male heir of the family in the second generation. It deprived the eldest son of nothing that would be his in accordance with the usual tenure of English primogeniture. Had he married and become the father of a family, his eldest son would have been the heir. But heretofore there had been no such entails in the Newton family; or, at least, he [Gregory] was pleased to think that there had been none such. And when he himself inherited the property early in life, – before he had reached his thirtieth year, – he thought that his father had injured him. His boy was as dear to him as though the mother had been his honest wife.   (I.127–8)

The male heir in the second generation is the parson's son, Ralph, Gregory's nephew. Gregory, sore that his beloved but illegitimate son will not inherit, is pleased to think that the land has descended in the family previously by will rather than entail, though one notices that here once again, though without an entail, the land has descended according to the principle of primogeniture as though there were an entail. Gregory's father, disgusted at the idea of a bastard possibly gaining possession, uses the entail to force his will on the descent of the property. Trollope fully exploits the ironies and tragedies that result. The legitimate heir, Ralph, is a feckless spendthrift desperately in need of money, and Gregory hopes that he may be able to buy the reversion from Ralph and give the land to his own son. He can do nothing else since he has only a life interest in the estate, the fee tail beginning with Ralph. The mystique of property and tradition mixes with prejudice about the status of bastards and shades of class discrimination, Ralph borrowing money from Neefit, a breeches-maker who appreciates the idea of a hereditary estate, on the understanding that Ralph

will marry Neefit's daughter, Polly. Gregory becomes obsessive
about the injustice:

> His thoughts were always dwelling on it, so that the whole
> peace and comfort of his life were disturbed. A life-interest
> in a property is, perhaps, as much as a man desires to have
> when he for whose protection he is debarred from further
> privileges of ownership is a well-loved son; – but an entail
> that limits an owner's rights on behalf of an heir who is not
> loved, who is looked upon as an enemy, is very grievous. And
> in this case the man who was so limited, so cramped, so
> hedged in, and robbed of the true pleasures of ownership,
> had a son with whom he would have been willing to share
> everything, – whom it would have been his delight to consult
> as to every roof to be built, every tree to be cut, every lease to
> be granted or denied. . . . As the sun is falling in the heavens
> and the evening lights come on, this world's wealth and
> prosperity afford no pleasure equal to this. It is this delight
> that enables a man to feel, up to the last moment, that the
> goods of the world are good. But of all this he was to be
> robbed. . . .   (I, 138–9)

Here is a typical instance of the way in which, for Trollope, the
law is no dry subject to be avoided but integral to his unfolding
drama, reaching from what is close at hand, a tree, a roof, a
gate, through the bonds of family and social relationship to the
whole network of sensibilities and associations that constitute
the feeling and identity of a nation or a race.

Criminal law brings us in touch with altogether more sensational activities, with horror and extremes, the stuff of jour-
nalism. Victorians, of course, had an Elizabethan streak in their
make-up in their fascination over grizzly, sordid, horrendous
crimes.[22] They enjoyed reading about a particularly ghastly
murder, discussed its fine points, and examined with critical
appreciation the whole conduct of the case and bearing of the
principal actors.[23] De Quincey parodies this enthusiasm in his
essay, 'Murder Considered as One of the Fine Arts'. The
Metropolitan Police Force was instituted in 1829 and the
system of a paid constabulary was extended to other towns until
an 1856 Act required all local authorities to create local police
forces. In 1842 the Commissioners of Metropolitan Police

established a Detective Department. Here was a new kind of expertise to add to the discriminating popular scholarship about criminal affairs. Dickens loved the detectives.[24] Whereas the early years of the period rejoiced in the Newgate novel,[25] concentrating on the violent exploits of the underworld – a taste continued at the base, common, and popular level by the pulpy thrillers of G. W. M. Reynolds – the 1850s saw the beginnings of detective fiction in works like Dickens's *Bleak House*, and Wilkie Collins's *The Moonstone*, though the pattern for detective ingenuity had been set by Poe's 'The Murders in the Rue Morgue'. Victorian interest in crime and detection, however, is not just the sign of a taste for vicarious sordidness and violence, a psychological compensation for the famous Victorian respectability. Detectives, in their attempts to ferret out truth by accumulating facts, are emblematic of the Victorian preoccupation with epistemology.[26] Everywhere in Victorian fiction, poetry, educational theory and philosophy, one finds an anxiety about facts, a thoroughly English empirical emphasis on the one hand and on the other a consciousness, after Hume's famous analysis of reason, that the worlds of facts and reason are divorced, that facts, so seemingly solid, are treacherous and unreliable. The work which most epitomises these concerns, linking the interpretation of a sordid crime with legalistic arguings, epistemological uncertainty, and the deceptive nature of language, is Browning's masterpiece, *The Ring and the Book*. A work in which Trollope shows similar interests is *He Knew He Was Right*.[27] Interpretation, often bizarre, about each other's motives, character, and actions, abounds between the protagonists as their marriage disintegrates. Louis Trevelyan hires an ex-policeman, Mr Bozzle, as a private investigator to spy on his wife. 'When I'm down on a fact, I am down on it,' declares Bozzle. 'Nothing else wouldn't do in my profession' (248). 'Facts is open, Mr. Trewillian, if you knows where to look for them' (592). Bozzle goes about, in a style we have come to recognise as universal among policemen, noting down facts, 'the smallest little,—tiddly things' in his memorandum book: 'Was let in at the front door on Friday the 5th by Sarah French, the housemaid, at 10.37 A.M., and was let out again by the same young woman at 11.41 A.M.' (221). Though Louis hates the 'odious details,—details not one of which possessed

the slightest importance' (222), though he 'felt that he was
defiling himself with dirt when he first went to Mr. Bozzle'
(179), and though his friend Hugh Stanbury urges him to rid
himself of Bozzle, he cannot sever himself from the abyss of
dark suspicion Bozzle represents.

> Mr. Bozzle was an active-minded man, who gloried in detect-
> ing, and who, in the special spirit of his trade, had taught
> himself to believe that all around him were things secret and
> hidden, which would be within his power of unravelling if
> only the slightest clue were put in his hand. He lived by the
> crookednesses of people, and therefore was convinced that
> straight doings in the world were quite exceptional. Things
> dark and dishonest, fights fought and races run that they
> might be lost, plants and crosses, women false to their
> husbands, sons false to their fathers, daughters to their
> mothers, servants to their masters, affairs always secret,
> dark, foul, and fraudulent, were to him the normal condition
> of life.   (268)

Like the others in the book, even Bozzle, the professional fact-
hunter, gets his facts wrong, makes the wrong interpretation
and assists in the downward spiral to distrust and disintegration.[28] His role is to provide the ocular proof. Trevelyan
'gave, in effect, the same order that Othello gave; – and Bozzle
went to work determined to obey it' (419). The proof, however,
is no sounder here than in *Othello*. As in Browning, what is seen
is relative to the mental probity of the viewer.
   Trollope's presentation of Bozzle, with his habitual cynicism,
his lower-class mannerisms and speech, suggests a nether
world meticulous in its catalogues of detail but claustrophobic,
insane, attuned to Trevelyan's creeping madness. It is a less
admiring, and no doubt, in some ways, truer portrait than that
of Dickens's Mr Bucket in *Bleak House*. Much of the human
discord in *He Knew He Was Right* is conveyed in conflicting
registers of expression used by the participants, as, for
example, in Bozzle's report to Trevelyan about his wife as 'a
lady as likes her fancy man' (421), unexceptionable language to
Bozzle, agony to Trevelyan's middle-class rectitude. But this is
Trollope, and even Bozzle has his good points. He dislikes the
job of snatching Trevelyan's child from his wife – 'it was his

business to find out facts, and not to perform actions' (492), and when the Revd Mr Outhouse, refusing him access to the child, orders him out, Bozzle 'was much impressed in favour of Mr. Outhouse, and would have been glad to have done that gentleman a kindness had an opportunity come in his way' (493).

In *The Eustace Diamonds*, Trollope presents Scotland Yard at work. With her limpet-like possessiveness, Lizzie Eustace refuses to give up the family diamonds after her husband's death. When her jewel box, without the diamonds, is stolen, she sees an opportunity to pretend she no longer has them and, giving a false deposition, allows the police to think them stolen. Later, they are in fact stolen, but to reveal the theft she would have to admit her previous lies, so she gives a second false deposition. Detective Gager, 'very clever, – almost too clever, and certainly a little too fast' (442), comes up with the theory of a double robbery, but he needs the evidence that Lizzie's maid, Patience Crabstick, now absconded, can provide. He resorts to extraordinary police methods, promising to marry her if she helps him: 'As soon as this work is off my mind, you shall be Mrs. Gager, my dear. And you'll be all right. You've been took in, that's what you have' (523). Connubiality and detection happily combine (though one wonders what he will do to solve his next case). At a higher level, Lizzie is persuaded to tell the truth about the diamonds by Major Mackintosh, chief of the London police. His tact overcomes her fear of prosecution for perjury:

> 'They will ask you to tell the truth.'
> 'Indeed I will do that,' said Lizzie, – not aware that, after so many lies, it might be difficult to tell the truth.
> 'And you will probably be asked to repeat it, this way and that, in a manner that will be troublesome to you. You see that here in London, and at Carlisle, you have – given incorrect versions.' (617)

'Incorrect versions' – the phrase is balm to Lizzie's larcenous, lying soul. 'Such a handsome man as he was, too.' The Major gets what he wants, 'escaping rather quickly from the room' (618–19), but even the magistrate is softened by Lizzie's pretty affectation of contrition. This is police work in a light key. The effect here, consonant with the whole brilliant tone of comic irony in the book, is of a sort of sombre amusement.

'The criminal law', Trollope says in *The New Zealander*, 'is to all of us the most important, as under it our lives, our property, and reputations are, or are supposed to be, secure' (54). Of the many reforms that occurred in Victorian criminal law, in codification, pleading, punishments, right to representation by counsel and so forth, one of the most important as it affects Trollope was the 1836 Act allowing defendants accused of felony the right to be represented by counsel – important because it made possible the category to which Trollope's most memorable barrister, seedy Mr Chaffanbrass of the Old Bailey, belongs, the barrister specialising in defence. As we shall see in the chapter on Chaffanbrass and the Old Bailey, Trollope had severe reservations about the function of the defence counsel, seeing him as a defender of villainy and confounder of truth. No doubt much of his information about criminal lawyers came from the newspapers, which reported the juicier Old Bailey trials.[29] In discussions about the reputation of lawyers in general, the point is often made by their defenders that the public tends to base its notions on the reported antics of criminal advocates at the Old Bailey, but that these stars hold rather a low status in the profession and are hardly to be taken as fair representatives of the profession as a whole. In *The New Zealander*, nevertheless, and in the person of bullying Mr Allwinde, Trollope polemically makes them so. Chaffanbrass is made in a similar mould. But despite apparent hostility, Trollope realises that he has a fine character in Chaffanbrass and by returning to him and thinking about him he eventually comes to a more enlightened understanding of the advocate's role.

By standing for election at Beverley and through his acquaintance with distinguished and influential lawyers, Trollope came to know a considerable amount about the law in relation to politics. The political world, of course, is a main resource for his novels. In the political as in the church novels, we see his keen interest in how society functions, both overtly and secretly in the inner realms of conscience and self-interest. By selecting from Trollope's gallery of lawyers, we can follow the whole career of the lawyer politician. In *The Life of Cicero*, we can examine the ideology. In *Ralph the Heir* and the Phineas novels, we can see the process of election and, since the elections there are corrupt, we see them in the light of nineteenth-century law on the subject. Among elected members Trollope also shows us, in several characters, the higher reaches of the law, Solicitors and Attorneys-General. And in *Lady Anna*, he presents what has been recognised as his most favourable impression of a lawyer, the Solicitor-General, Sir William Patterson.[30]

A topic of legal interest to which Trollope devotes frequent attention, if not as much as to the inheritance and management of estates, is the disabilities of women. His personal attitudes, as typified by such comments as 'The necessity of the supremacy of man is as certain to me as the eternity of the soul,'[31] or, of Alice Vavasor's questionings, 'What should a woman do with her life? . . . Fall in love, marry the man, have two children, and live happy ever afterwards' (*CYFH*, I, 134), are well known and much written about.[32] Nevertheless, he is peculiarly interesting on the subject because of his unusual gift for imagining and dramatically presenting the opposing view. His many women who bear the weight of frustration and resentment under such an ideology as he himself adheres to, who chafe, rebel, or find indirect means of realising their aspirations in a world rigged against them, are among his most vital and sympathetic creations. The questions of women's rights and abilities was, of course, a major topical concern of the early Victorian period, reaching a special degree of intensity in the time when he wrote his major novels. Tennyson on women's education (*The Princess*), Ruskin on women as goddesses of the hearth, Huxley on the emancipation of women in the light of their evolutionary condition, Harriet Taylor on the 'Enfranchisement of Women', and John Stuart Mill on *The Subjection of Women* are only eminent examples of a much wider range of interest, discussion and publication.[33] Like Mill (who for his support of women's interests receives satirical mention several times in Trollope's works), Trollope is interested in the complex interactions of individuals within the legal framework of society. Here again, interest was keen. In 1854 as a result of her own notorious sufferings, Caroline Norton published a pamphlet on *English Laws for Women in the Nineteenth Century*, and Barbara Leigh Smith one entitled *A Brief Summary in Plain Language, of the Most Important Laws Concerning Women*. In 1857 the famous Divorce Act was passed. And between 1857 and 1882, eighteen Bills were presented to Parliament on the subject of married women's property.[34]

Unmarried women and widows had the general ideology of

male dominance to contend with. When George Vavasor in *Can You Forgive Her?* tries to cash a bill signed by his sister Alice, he finds that he cannot because 'the City, by one of its mouths, asserted plainly that ladies' bills never meant business' (II, 255). But under Common Law, when a woman married, her real property and the income from it came under her husband's control, and her personal property became his. She could not dispose of her real property by a will, and he could do whatever he pleased with what had been her personal property. If he died first, her real property reverted to her, and under the practice of dower a life interest in one-third of her husband's lands became hers. (An 1833 statute allowed her husband to set aside her dower rights.) Frequently a dower house was provided to which the widow removed upon the death of her husband so that the elder son, or next male in line, could take over the mansion. There is a great bother about the dower house in *Is He Popenjoy?* where the outrageous Marquis tells his mother and sisters to quit the neighbourhood though his mother has a right to the dower house which he has rented. The consequences of such laws are everywhere in Trollope's books. As J. S. McMaster points out in her discussion of the men and women in his novels, 'The young Lady Glencora, who is an heiress on an immense scale, not only sees her whole fortune automatically alienated to her husband's estate, but is expected to endure lectures from his friends on her extravagance in keeping out his horses – (fortunately she does not endure it).'[35] Glencora, who also suffers from the frustration of a woman kept out of the world of affairs, is able to relieve that frustration, influencing them indirectly, by managing splendid entertainments for her husband's political associates with the argument that she is using only the money she brought to their marriage. In *The Way We Live Now*, Marie Melmotte, daughter of a notorious financier, eventually marries an American, Mr Fisker: 'She had contrived to learn that, in the United States, a married woman has greater power over her own money than in England, and this information acted strongly in Fisker's favour' (II, 453). One of the major occupations in Trollope's novels, as in the novels of his mentor Thackeray, is fortune hunting in the marriage market.[36] With Glencora and Palliser arrangements are on the grand scale, but the hunt is pursued with greater anxiety and a good deal of class tension at lower levels – usually a case of a down-at-heel aristocrat or member of the gentry condescending to marry a wealthy commoner. For the ordinary individual, like Jack De Baron in *Is He Popenjoy?*, marriage with a reasonably wealthy woman (he estimates £20 000 will do) is a necessity for a decent life. On a grander scale, it represents consolidation of power and status in society. Trollope not only describes a society in which these conditions prevail, but makes them the object of articulate and brooding preoccupation and discussion among his characters.

The way for a woman to avoid appropriation of her property by her husband was through a marriage settlement, which could designate property, whether real or personal, as her separate property. These arrangements, according to the principles of equity rather than of common law, allowed her to receive income from her estate and spend it, incur debts on it, sue or be sued about it, and give it away, sell it, or bequeath it without her husband's permission. As in a duel, seconds (lawyers and parents) were important in negotiating the agreements – consider Hogarth's *Marriage à la Mode*, where the parents haggle in the foreground, one bargaining for money to build a mansion, the other for nobility to pass on to his descendants. Trollope shows us some of this, in *Is He Popenjoy?* and *Mr Scarborough's Family*, for example, but one supposes his sympathies lie with Daniel Thwaite of *Lady Anna*, who, though a radical, is determined that his wife will have no property of her own. In *Mr Scarborough's Family*, extensive bargaining occurs between the two sets of lawyers for Matilda Thoroughbung (from a wealthy brewer's family) and Mr Prosper, but, as we shall see, Trollope handles the whole matter comically, including Mr Prosper's shocked discovery that Matilda is ready to override the lawyers' opinions on the grounds that women's rights are 'coming up'. It would take someone like Miss Thoroughbung or Lady Glencora to benefit from such a settlement, however, since only wealthy women could afford the protection of equity.

A characteristic Trollopian treatment of such concerns occurs in *Is He Popenjoy?*, where issues of masculine dominance, inheritance, money versus family status, marriage for profit, dower rights and legitimacy are the very essence of the novel, though no one in this instance goes to actual litigation.

Lord George Germain is a rather brooding, stuffy character, 'so grim, so gaunt, so sombre' (I, 2), a penurious younger son left to act as steward to the estate and caretaker of his mother and five sisters while his elder brother, the Marquis, lives a dissolute life in Italy. George conveniently marries Mary, the daughter of Dean Lovelace, whose father, to the great distaste of the Germain family, had kept livery stables at Bath. The Dean is well off and Mary has also had money left to her. George, however, is a snob. 'Our rank is high', he says of himself and his sisters, 'and our means are small. But to me blood is much more than wealth' (I, 49). To his surprise, his brother marries and claims to have a son, whereupon Lord George thinks uncomfortably: 'But now he would only be his wife's husband, the Dean's son-in-law, living on their money, and compelled by circumstances to adapt himself to them' (I, 129). He is much given to thoughts about 'the grandeur of his family' (I, 250), and to this vanity he adds convictions about 'his divine superiority' as a husband (a phrase oft-repeated in the novel). Among the stipulations the Dean makes before the marriage is one that the married couple are to spend several months of the year in a house provided in London. George is tied to his sisters and to the family estate, however, and resents the London interludes. When in London, he resents his wife becoming friends with Captain Jack De Baron, also in search of a woman with a fortune, but himself becomes enmeshed with a married woman. 'He did like spending his own time with Mrs. Houghton, but it was dreadful to him to think that his wife should be spending hers with Jack De Baron' (I, 249). Trollope writes a very shrewd study of the counterbalancing resentments and self-justifications that erode a marriage, and in the course of it satirises the double standard and the notion of husbandly godliness. 'His stronghold was that of marital authority – authority unbounded, legitimate, and not to be questioned' (II, 114). His own shortcomings, however, cause him some embarrassment. 'He was, he was sure, quite right as to that theory about Caesar's wife, even though, from the unfortunate position of circumstances, he could not dilate upon it at the present moment' (II, 15). Though he thinks, 'What a man does is different' (II, 74), his position is weak: 'Now, when a man assumes the divine superiority of an all-governing husband, his own hands should be quite clean' (II, 17).

Things become worse when it looks as though George will
not ever be Marquis. His scandalous brother claims to have a
son and writes telling George, his mother and sisters, not only
to clear out of the family mansion but not to use the dower
house. To George's greater annoyance, the Dean, with all that
taint of the stables, takes up his cause (or rather the cause of
his daughter's possible son, who might become Marquis) and
puts lawyers on to finding out if, as seems likely, the Marquis's
son is illegitimate. Questions of property, legitimacy, who
brings what to a marriage, and what feelings result, dominate
the novel and combine with Trollope's usual concern about
the possession and administration of estates. They also merge
with the more general theme of authority within marriage in
the nicely balanced extra-marital relationships of George and
Mary. Indeed, one almost feels an anticipation of the 1960s as
Mrs Houghton tells George:

> 'There are five or six of us playing this little comedy. Mr.
> Houghton and I are married, but we have not very much to
> say to each other. It is the same with you and Mary.'
> 'I deny it.'
> 'I dare say; but at the same time you now it to be true. She
> consoles herself with Captain De Baron. With whom Mr.
> Houghton consoles himself I have never taken the trouble
> to inquire. I hope someone is good-natured to him, poor
> old soul. Then, as to you and me, you used, I think, to get
> consolation here. But such comforts cost trouble, and you
> hate trouble.'   (II, 30)

George eventually learns a little by experience and gets out of
Mrs Houghton's game. As Mrs Montacute Jones tells Mary,
'When grown people play at being children, it is apt to be
dangerous' (II, 62). And as for husbandly divinity, Trollope
suggests that, at least in emotional economics, some equality is
necessary in marriage. A wife, he says, 'never feels that all the
due privileges of her life have been accorded to her till her
husband shall have laid himself open to the caresses of a
pardon. Then, and not till then, he is her equal; and equality is
necessary for comfortable love' (I, 315).

A Victorian case that attracted a great deal of attention to
the cruelties women suffered under the law was that of

Caroline Norton, whose husband charged Lord Melbourne with adultery with her. She separated from Norton in 1836 but could not obtain a divorce. Though much of her property became Norton's under common law, he refused to pay her a tolerable allowance after the separation, and when she turned to writing to support herself, he sought possession of her earnings. Among the more outrageous acts by which he exercised his masculine prerogatives, having all the rights of custody under common law, he abducted her children, refusing to let her see them. Trollope touches on the matter of custody in *He Knew He Was Right*, where Louis Trevelyan, suffering from pathological jealousy, and with the aid of his private detective, Bozzle, abducts his child from his wife, and there is little she can do about it. Proving Louis mad turns out to be very difficult.

As Lee Holcombe observes in an excellent essay on 'Victorian Wives and Property', the famous Divorce Bill of 1857 took the wind out of the sails of the Married Women's Property Bill, but ironically Sir Thomas Erskine Perry, Liberal MP for Devonport submitted such a bill in 1857 in the hope that 'the passage of his measure would prevent that of the Divorce Bill, which he thought would lead to the "corruption of morals"' (3 Hansard, CXLV, 268).[37] In *The Three Clerks* (1858), Charley Tudor, who hopes to be a writer and has just finished one of his first pieces, gets some advice from his editor:

> 'We have polished off poison and petticoats pretty well,' said the editor; 'what do you say to something political?'
> Charley had no objection in life.
> 'This Divorce Bill, now – we could have half a dozen married couples all separating, getting rid of their ribs and buckling again, helter-skelter, every man to somebody else's wife; and the parish parson refusing to do the work; just to show the immorality of the thing.' (547)

Despite the sensitivity with which Trollope portrays the frustrations of women under the law, he depicts the women's rights movement in general in a comic and satirical light as when the American ambassador in Florence buttonholes Lord Glascock in *He Knew He Was Right* for an argument on the virtues of that remarkable man, Mr Mill, who 'has understood that women must at last be put upon an equality with men' (521), or in his account of the 'Rights of Women Institute. Established for the Relief of the Disabilities of Females' in *Is He Popenjoy?*.

> By friendly tongues to friendly ears, 'The College' or 'The Institute' was the pleasant name used; but the irreverent public was apt to speak of the building generally as 'The Female Disabilities'. And the title was made even shorter. Omnibuses were desired to stop at the 'Disabilities'.   (I, 159)

Of Mary's expected child Mrs Montacute Jones writes, 'Only how the bonfires wouldn't burn if it should turn out to be only a disability after all' (II, 250). Nevertheless, though Trollope's own conservative attitudes are plain, his imaginative depiction of women's disabilities and frustrated aspirations, especially in cases such as that of Lady Laura Standish in the Palliser series, is sensitive and moving. The women who rebel against his own convictions are the liveliest in his work.

Finally, we must look at Trollope's handling of relationships between lawyers, or more especially, between the branches of the profession. The two branches differ in function, education and status. Barristers, with sole right to plead in the higher courts, live in London and consider themselves the cream of the profession. Solicitors, though they are the ones who initially see the lay clients and are in fact the family lawyers, had before our period a chequered history and a comparatively low status. From the eighteenth century, their societies were concerned to improve their education and status and protect their interests *vis à vis* the barristers. By the Victorian period, their reputation had risen considerably. Several points of contention were being aired, however, and they are reflected in Trollope's novels. As we shall see, there was lively contemporary debate about the etiquette of who saw clients. The lay client ordinarily saw the solicitor who then briefed a barrister, but the issue was hotly disputed, and Trollope exploits it comically in *Orley Farm*, where sweetly pathetic Lady Mason resorts directly to the sympathetic shoulder of distinguished but susceptible Mr Furnival, a barrister.

Status within the branches of the Victorian profession has

several dimensions. In general, barristers are gentlemen. Solicitors may be. Mr Prosper in *Mr Scarborough's Family*, serene in the confidence that his own solicitor, Mr Grey, is a gentleman, is sorely troubled at having to communicate with such low fellows as Miss Thoroughbung's attorneys, Soames and Simpson. Slow and Bideawhile, who recur in several novels, are intensely respectable, but upstarts like Squercum in *The Way We Live Now*, with no natural respect for the dignity of fathers over sons, are sharp practicers. Barristers also differ in status. If barristers are the cream of the profession, Chancery barristers consider themselves the *crème de la crème*. Lady Glencora, plotting theatrical strategies and pressure to aid Phineas Finn when he is charged with murder, acknowledges to Mr Low that such things are not countenanced in Chancery. At the opposite extreme perhaps are the criminal barristers of the Old Bailey like Trollope's savage Mr Chaffanbrass, popular stars but not noted in the profession itself for prestige or learning. Mr Dove, of *The Eustace Diamonds*, is another sort of barrister, a great scholar with an infectious belief in the poetry of the law. As we have seen, lawyers are important for better or worse in the machinery of government, and Trollope shows us lawyers at all stages of combined legal and political careers, from relative nobodies like Frank Greystock to gentlemen of the 'right sort' like the suave Solicitor-General, Sir William Patterson. Though Trollope, with some notable exceptions, writes rather caustically of lawyers, he, like Lady Glencora, gives judges a proper degree of veneration. Unfortunately, they do not figure very largely in his fiction. Judge Staveley in *Orley Farm* is a kind and admirable figure, but except for some beneficial influence that he exerts on the priggish young barrister, Felix Graham, he is not seen in a professional capacity.

Law is a machinery of courts, statutes and professional practitioners – but it is also an idea. Justice, as distinguished from law, but also in relation to it or in tension with it, has occupied some of the greatest minds and works of western culture. Job resorts to forensic language with God, and trials are a major motif in literature from the *Oresteia* to *King Lear* to Kafka's *The Trial*. It is not always easy to discriminate what should be rendered to Caesar and what to God, to know what law is or which law should be obeyed. Trollope, as we all know, is the novelist of the ordinary. His world is not the elemental or phantasmagoric world of *King Lear* or *The Trial*. But along with the society he depicts he inherits ideas of law that are part of elaborate philosophical traditions. He frequently resorts to ideas of truth, and of inner light in the perception of truth, that should go along with the notion of natural law, the idea that mundane laws are reflections of divine law. Bentham and his nineteenth-century followers, however, took a very harsh view of such appeals to the extra-terrestrial. And one or two of Trollope's more iconoclastic characters call conventional notions of law and law-abidingness in question with entertainingly outrageous results. Though I shall for the most part be dealing with the down-to-earth context of nineteenth-century laws and lawyers, in the final chapter on *Mr Scarborough's Family* I shall address the philosophical traditions Trollope puts in tension there.

To conclude, Trollope may not have had Dickens's opportunities to observe the legal system, or certain parts of the legal system, in operation and few people ever had Dickens's fly-paper sensibility on which anything that landed stuck. Holdsworth in his great history of English law and in his book on *Dickens as Legal Historian* is right to give Dickens major treatment as a sharp-eyed recorder of legal scenes and practices. And one understands why Holdsworth gives attention to Samuel Warren, a barrister, whose novel *Ten Thousand a Year* gives interesting insights into the law, though hardly anyone reads it. But given the scale and imbedded importance of law and lawyers in Trollope's fiction, given the way he treats law as an impressive part of the whole intricate network of psychological and administrative forces making up a functioning society, Trollope, perhaps, deserved some mention.

2 Sex in the Barrister's Chambers: Lawyer and Client in *Orley Farm*

'The truth, the whole truth, and nothing but the truth.' The familiar courtroom oath expresses one of Trollope's major ideals, but as he moves from assertion to imaginative exploration of the ideal, he finds, like other Victorians, that truth is very hard to grasp. In *Orley Farm* he attacks the legal system and lawyers because, while organised to search out the truth, they seem to Trollope willfully to confound it. In the original reviews and subsequently, lawyers and literary critics have often addressed themselves to his management of legal issues, largely with a view to setting him straight, particularly on the ethics of advocacy, terminology, and procedure in trials.[1] Nevertheless, between Robert Polhemus's view that 'Trollope presents, on the whole in *Orley Farm*, a fair and illuminating picture of the legal system,'[2] and the verdict of the reviewer (one suspects, a barrister) who concluded 'Mr Trollope knows nothing whatever of the subject on which he is so vehement,'[3] we find quite a range of opinion.

What has received only passing comment is, perhaps, what Trollope does best in the management of law in the novel, what we might expect him to do best, the intricate personal and professional relationship of lawyer and client, more particularly the relationship of Mr Furnival, barrister and MP, and Lady Mason. Here Trollope is on solid, if not very technical, ground, with a special system of professional etiquette, the code governing appointment and conference between client, solicitor and barrister, within which to place a complicating drama of sexual hunger and manipulation. The English reader, alert to the division and methods of the

English legal profession, would be more likely than the North American reader to notice something odd about these conferences. Whatever Trollope's views about the abstract question of defending the guilty, and they are decidedly reactionary, his knowledge of etiquette among lawyers and clients is sound enough, and he uses it repeatedly to point up a complex moral and emotional tangle. Mr Furnival's aberrations rise credibly from barely acknowledged urges that Trollope examines with all his skill for nuance, perversity and contradiction in character.

The principal thread of the plot (put briefly and ignoring the legal objections about its possibility) has to do with Lady Mason's forging a codicil of her dead husband's will so as to ensure that her son, Lucius, rather than her husband's son by a previous marriage, Joseph Mason of Groby Park, inherits Orley Farm. The codicil is unsuccessfully contested, and twenty years later, on her son's coming of age, Lady Mason turns over the farm to him. He reclaims fields long rented to a mean-spirited solicitor, Samuel Dockwrath, who, in revenge, re-explores the will, comes up with new evidence, and successfully instigates a new trial of Lady Mason on a charge of perjury. As rumour of his machinations grows, Lady Mason consults Mr Furnival, a barrister of some note, who acted for her in the first case.

The relationship between Lady Mason and Mr Furnival, in fact, occupies a considerable portion of the novel and is psychologically explored in a variety of tones both sad and amusing. Even more than her eventual relationship with Sir Peregrine Orme, whom she rather reluctantly consents to marry, knowing that his social prestige will do a great deal to buttress her respectability and status in the community, her relationship with Mr Furnival shows Trollope developing a character, and the novel, on two levels. His problem was to present a guilty woman as quasi-heroine without offending the ethical standards of his readership. Though her guilt is not to be revealed until fairly late in the novel, he expects, as he then says, that 'Lady Mason's confession . . . will not have taken anybody by surprise' (II, 42). Still, she grows on Trollope to the extent that at the end he may, he says, 'owe an apology to my readers in that I have asked their sympathy for a woman who had so sinned as to have placed her beyond the general sympathy of the world at large' (II, 404). For the virtuous reader, he has her indulge in rather a lot of repentant writhing and 'hiding her face upon the floor' (II, 355). Moreover, he tells us from the start that though 'Women for the most part are prone to love-making – as nature has intended that they should be; . . . there are women from whom all such follies seem to be as distant as skittles and beer are distant from the dignity of the Lord Chancellor. Such a woman was Lady Mason' (I, 19). For the more evil-minded reader, the one who reads James's *The Turn of the Screw* as Wilson and Goddard read it, more as a psychological fable than as a simple ghost story, there is another Lady Mason. And the English reader would perhaps begin to suspect that things were a little peculiar as soon as Lady Mason, having summoned Mr Furnival all the way from an international conference of lawyers in Birmingham, consults him in his chambers in Lincoln's Inn.

Mr Furnival is a barrister, and according to legal etiquette lay clients do not consult barristers directly but only through a solicitor.[4] Narrowly speaking, the solicitor is the barrister's client. The solicitor manages the general conduct of the case and engages whatever barrister seems likely, under the circumstances, to plead the case most effectively in court. Solicitors had repeatedly tried in the eighteenth and nineteenth centuries to ensure that even clients who only wished advice should get it, not from barristers, but from them. Harry Kirk in his authoritative survey of the solicitors' profession says that, among the various matters of contention between solicitors and barristers in the nineteenth century, the issue 'which caused the most heart-burning and aroused a great deal of public interest and on occasion some plain speaking from the general press' was the right of barristers to take instructions directly from the public without the intervention of solicitors or attorneys.[5] Kirk succinctly describes the salient opinions and outbursts. Having in 1762 talked of prosecution to enforce the etiquette, in 1800 the Society of Gentlemen Practisers (that is, solicitors) reiterated: 'It was a highly improper practice for counsel to receive clients and transact their business independently and without the intervention of an attorney.'[6] Barristers, nevertheless, occasionally resisted. In 1842 Lord Brougham defied a boycott by attorneys of the northern circuit, saying no rule could be found to prohibit his accepting instructions directly from laymen. The wording of the County Courts Act of 1846 seemingly forbade barristers from taking instructions directly from a lay client, but in an appeal contesting the point in 1850, though Lord Chief Justice Campbell observed that the etiquette was no rule of law ('the etiquette of the Bar is one thing; a practice which is to bind the world is another'), he nevertheless expressed the hope that barristers would 'continue generally to adhere to what has been the etiquette of the Bar'.[7] And in 1862, the year *Orley Farm* was published, Serjeant Pulling, says Kirk,

> in his standard work on the Law of Attorneys gave the most balanced view: 'During the last century the practice was gradually introduced of barristers requiring the intervention of attorneys and solicitors in cases which came professionally before them . . . ; and such is the practice now generally followed though the legal right of barristers to dispense with such interventions is unquestionable.'[8]

Public sentiment, arising from the presumption that one fee was better than two, was generally against the etiquette, as in thunderous articles in *The Times* for 1 and 7 November, 1851. The *Cornhill Magazine* in 1863 (p.111), on the other hand, questioned the supposed economy of direct access. Nevertheless the etiquette prevailed. Kirk observes: 'the hard fact was that if the Bar had taken instructions direct from clients it would have become indistinguishable from the attorneys and solicitors and would have ceased to exist as a separate profession.'[9] The issue, though not sensational or inflammatory by some standards, was a matter of public and professional contention, carried on not only in professional journals and papers like the *Law Times* and the *Law Magazine and Review* but in public forums like *The Times* and the *Cornhill Magazine*. Trollope, in raising the issue in *Orley Farm*, therefore, is exploiting one of the more notorious general concerns about the practice of law in the nineteenth century, and though few writers in the debate might have stressed exactly the perils to the barrister that Trollope dwells upon, they might have been sympathetic to the implication that barristers who see lay clients directly are likely to lose some of the

objectivity in handling a case that having solicitors in the front
line between the public and them permits.

Even with a solicitor, seeing the barrister was not to be taken
for granted:

> 'See Serjeant Snubbin, my dear sir!' rejoined Perker [to Mr.
> Pickwick], in utter amazement. 'Pooh, pooh, my dear sir,
> impossible. See Serjeant Snubbin! Bless you, my dear sir,
> such a thing was never heard of, without a consultation fee
> being previously paid, and a consultation fixed. It couldn't
> be done, my dear sir; it couldn't be done.'[10]

So, although Lady Mason's direct approach to the barrister is
not unheard of – she claims Mr Furnival as a friend, and Lord
Brougham himself, as noted in *Bennet* v. *Hale*, had acted for a
penurious friend without a solicitor[11] – it is unusual. That is
why Mr Furnival, in connubial conversation, and apart from
his attraction to Lady Mason, affects ignorance of her
impending visit to his chambers, though he tells himself that
his secrecy is a matter of professional confidentiality: 'The
reader,' says Trollope,

> will of course observe that this deceit was practised, not as
> between husband and wife with reference to an assignation
> with a lady, but between the lawyer and the outer world with
> reference to a private meeting with a client. But then it is
> sometimes so difficult to make wives look at such matters in
> the right light.   (I, 111–12)

Lady Mason arrives dressed with fetching and studied plain-
ness. An almost Pumblechookian degree of hand holding
takes place (six times during the interview by my count) with
dashes in the text to make us linger on their interpretation:
'And he again took her hand, – that he might encourage her'
(I, 117). She weeps devastatingly:

> Her tears were not false as Mr. Furnival well saw; and seeing
> that she wept, and seeing that she was beautiful, and feeling
> that in her grief and in her beauty she had come to him for
> aid, his heart was softened towards her, and he put out his
> arms as though he would take her to his heart – as a
> daughter.   (I, 122)

Clearly this is not the convention Vice-Chancellor Megarry refers to in *Lawyer and Litigant in England* when he says of the barrister: 'Clients rarely get close enough to his shoulder to weep on it, whether metaphorically or otherwise.'[12] Just at this moment, however, Mrs Furnival arrives, seething with jealousy, makes a scene, and flounces out, slamming the door behind her. Lady Mason apologises for being in the way:

> 'I know that barristers do not usually allow themselves to be troubled by their clients in their own chambers.'
> 'Nor by their wives,' Mr. Furnival might have added, but he did not.   (I, 126)

She too knows the etiquette. There is in fact little but rumour of Dockwrath's machinations for Lady Mason to consult Furnival about as yet. And it is no doubt significant that the one piece of substance in the interview is dropped in almost as an afterthought by Lady Mason apropos of the pains of suffering another trial:

> 'If you can save me from that, even though it be by the buying off of that ungrateful man—'
> 'You must not think of that.'
> 'Must I not? ah me!'   (I, 127)

Lady Mason is a master of the innocent 'ah me!'. She is, of course, playing the helpless female, pretending that the nature of what she has suggested, bribery to cover up a possible crime, is all too much for little her. Her work with tears and hands concludes neatly as she departs:

> with some further pressing of the hand, and further words of encouragement which were partly tender as from the man, and partly forensic as from the lawyer, Mr. Furnival permitted her to go, and she found her son at the chemist's shop in Holborn as she had appointed. There were no traces of tears or of sorrow in her face as she smiled on Lucius while giving him her hand. . . .   (I, 128)

'Tender as from the man, forensic as from the lawyer' puts Furnival's ambiguous state of mind dexterously. His forensic powers are under the control, not of professional judgement, but of sexual attraction. His client governs him. And Lady Mason, likewise ambiguous in her feelings – we are to understand that her manipulation of Furnival is almost unconscious – consults him as a lawyer but with a body language that, artfully or not, speaks to him as an admirer. Trollope was fond of the Ovidian tag about seeing the better way and taking the worse, and one of his variations on the expression fits Furnival like a glove: 'Men are unable to fathom their own desires, and fail to govern themselves by the wisdom which is at their fingers' ends' (*LC*, I, 345).[13]

Furnival as lawyer, says Trollope, 'was a safe man, understanding his trade, true to his clients, and very damaging as an opponent' (I, 95). His expertise, unlike that of Mr Chaffanbrass, champion of criminal cases at the Old Bailey, is broad and deep: 'He had been employed on abstruse points of law. . . . Indeed there is no branch of the Common Law in which he was not regarded as great and powerful. . . . Mr. Furnival's reputation has spread itself wherever stuff gowns and horsehair wigs are held in estimation' (I, 97). He is also an MP, member for the Essex Marshes. Why, then, does he permit himself to be manoeuvred by pretty demonstrations of woe? It is not just that 'his eye loved to look upon the beauty of a lovely woman, his ear loved to hear the tone of her voice, and his hand loved to meet the soft ripeness of her touch'(I, 252), though he *has* been 'obtaining for himself among other successes the character of a Lothario' (I, 99). No, he is a rather acute example of a special Trollopian syndrome, the masculine problem of dealing with age fifty or thereabouts. In his *Thackeray*, Trollope notes with interest how Thackeray at that age spoke 'as though the world were all behind him instead of before' (49–50). Thackeray himself said, 'At 47 Venus may rise from the sea, and I for one should hardly put on my spectacles to have a look.'[14] Trollope, however, seems rather afraid that he might, and that it would be both ridiculous and improper. Some friends, he says, 'told me that at fifty-five I ought to give up the fabrication of love-stories' (342). And his characters come under a similar interdiction. John Ball, who at least succeeds in marrying the heroine of *Miss Mackenzie*, is already, at no more than 'somewhat past forty', 'bald-headed, stout' and an 'ancient Romeo' (74, 88). Colonel Osborne in *He*

Knew He Was Right, who being 'past fifty' might be considered
'a safe friend for a young married woman' (5), nevertheless
impotently fosters and relishes the reputation of a marriage-
breaker. It can be said of him as of Tappitt, the brewer in
Rachel Ray, who is considered a 'very old man', that 'men of
fifty-five do not like to be so regarded, and are not anxious to
be laid upon shelves by their juniors' (168). William Whittle-
staff, in *An Old Man's Love,* proposes at fifty to a twenty-five-
year-old but renounces her to a younger lover. Mr Prosper in
Mr Scarborough's Family, at an unprepossessing fifty, makes a
fool of himself by proposing to Matilda Thoroughbung just to
annoy and disinherit his nephew. In short, men in their fifties
are to Trollope sexually troublesome both to themselves and
others. The love interest is best conducted by the youthfully
nubile. But Mr Furnival's case is peculiarly complicated.
Professionally he is at his peak because, says Trollope, 'barristers did not come to their prime till a period of life at which
other men are supposed to be in their decadence' (I, 95).
Maritally he is restless because the wife who pleased him when
they were young no longer pleases him in his eminence – like
Tennyson's Ulysses, he feels himself unhappily 'Match'd with
an aged wife', though both he and his wife are fifty-five. And
his own age and hard work show: 'Not that he was becoming
old, or weak, or worn; but his eye had lost its fire – except the
fire peculiar to his profession' (I, 96). In the popular jargon of
our own time, we might say that Mr Furnival is suffering an
acute case of male menopause. The subterranean disturb-
ances in Furnival's psyche make him an especially interesting
part of Trollope's display of legal delinquency, a display
which, in its theory of how lawyers in general behave in their
profession, is nonsense. We can believe in Mr Furnival,
however, because we see why he is moved to behave so
eccentrically. The forensic and the sexual are at odds in him:
'The advice to be given was to a widowed woman from an
experienced man of the world; but, nevertheless, he could
only make his calculations as to her peculiar case in the way in
which he ordinarily calculated' (I, 118–19). These calculations, however, involve the question of her innocence or guilt,
and that is a question he cannot bring himself to ask. The
forensic and sexual are apparent again in his professional
bemusement at the thought that Lady Mason forged the will

'so skilfully as to have baffled lawyers and jurymen . . . was it not all wonderful! Had she not been a woman worthy of wonder!' (I,130–1).

Though the course of seduction is very plain, even at times quite comic, Trollope takes care to suggest that it is barely conscious, interspersing his comments with qualifiers: 'seems', 'perhaps', the silent hesitation of dashes, and Trollope's customary signal of disingenuousness, 'he taught himself'. But despite his discretion, Trollope manages a tonality that communicates the imperative sexual urgency leading Furnival astray. We are told, in the general summary of Furnival's career, that 'he, at the age of fifty-five, was now running after strange goddesses' (I, 99). Trollope, of course, expects an educated reader to catch the biblical echo and remember the original recurrent phrase about the children of Israel in Judges: 'And yet they would not hearken unto their judges, but they went a whoring after other gods.'[15] The same hanky-panky occurs in Exodus; and in Kings, where Solomon 'loved many strange women' and 'his wives turned away his heart after other gods.'[16] The point is always the same sexual indictment: seductive women leading men from the true faith as Furnival is led from professional wisdom and honesty. Trollope too makes a refrain of the phrase 'running after strange goddesses' and puts it through its paces: 'tempted . . . to stray after strange goddesses' (I, 115); 'As though he had taken to himself in very truth some strange goddess' (I, 129); and 'Mr. Furnival's taste with reference to strange goddesses was beginning to be understood by the profession' (I, 169). Just as Furnival suppresses from consciousness a clear sense of what is impelling him, Trollope maintains a decorous surface by repeating a delicate phrase that, nevertheless, cannot but remind us quietly of the original trenchant term, 'whoring'.

Furnival does not, in fact, know that Lady Mason is guilty. He presumes it, and comes to feel increasingly convinced. If he were certain (and Trollope makes no such discrimination), it would be proper for him to decline the case and advise her to see an attorney. He cannot bring himself to do that.

He laid out for himself no scheme of wickedness with reference to her; he purposely entertained no thoughts which he knew to be wrong; but, nevertheless, he did feel that he liked to have her by him . . . that he liked to wipe the tears from those eyes [and] feel the pressure of that hand.   (I, 251)

Though it is a lawyer's duty to be frank to his client and discourage litigation, Furnival is now hamstrung.[17] When the question of whether the case can be won eventually arises, 'he must now either assure her by a lie, or break down all her hopes by the truth. . . Should he now be honest to his friend, or dishonest?' Pretending to himself that the support of Sir Peregrine, who is present at the interview, is necessary, 'he looked the lie' (I, 262–3). He fails, thus, both as friend and counsel.

Having confounded his roles as counsel, friend and swain, Furnival is enmeshed in a web of ironies when he finally comes to consider for himself the etiquette of how this case must be handled:

It would be necessary, if the case did come to a trial, that she should employ some attorney. The matter must come into the barrister's hands in the usual way, through a solicitor's house, and it would be well that the person employed should have a firm faith in his client. What could he say – he, as a barrister – if the attorney suggested to him that the lady might possibly be guilty? As he thought of all these things he almost dreaded the difficulties before him.   (I, 253)

It is not just that Furnival has put himself in an awkward position, as anyone might, by indulging a friend; as his wife uncomfortably reminds him, he has betrayed what he firmly accepts and expounds as a professional principle: 'Ladies don't go to barristers' chambers about law business. All that is done by attorneys. I've heard you say scores of times that you never would see people themselves. . . .' (II, 86). Poor Furnival! His whole tangled web of amatory, marital, and legal interests moves relentlessly towards farce, as Trollope's labyrinthine turn of language suggests: 'He must settle what attorney should have the matter in hand, and instruct that attorney how to reinstruct him, and how to reinstruct those other barristers who must necessarily be employed on the defence, in a case of such magnitude' (I, 341). Indeed, at one point, he is almost ready to say the hell with it. He himself has encouraged Lady Mason to cultivate Sir Peregrine Orme's neighbourly friendship for the sake of respectability by association, and, though suspicious, has been complacent: 'Sir Peregrine looked as though he were her father as he took her hand, and the barrister immediately comforted himself with the remembrance of the baronet's great age' (I, 261). Now, not only has Furnival come ever closer to being convinced of her guilt, but the aged Sir Peregrine (not a mere fifty-five, he's over seventy) has proposed to Lady Mason and been accepted. What a mess! Mr Furnival 'began to wish that he had never seen Lady Mason, and to reflect that the intimate friendship of pretty women often brings with it much trouble. He was resolved on one thing. He would not go down into court and fight that battle for Lady Orme' (I, 408).

However, he persuades her that 'it would create in men's minds . . . a strong impression against you, were you to marry him at this moment' (II, 8), and she, for her own reasons, is ready to be persuaded.

So, who are the solicitors to be? He goes through the form of considering Slow and Bideawhile, Sir Peregrine's attorneys and like Sir Peregrine immensely respectable, but 'Old Slow would not conceal the truth for all the baronets in England – no, nor for all the pretty women' (I, 263). Having abandoned professional scruple, Furnival now has to yield even on his class and racial prejudices. Chaffanbrass, formidable despite his taint of the Old Bailey, suggests Solomon Aram.

> 'Isn't he a Jew?'
> 'Upon my word I don't know. He's an attorney, and that's enough for me.'   (I, 345)

Furnival, who feels 'it would be a disgrace to him to take a case out of Solomon Aram's hands', concludes 'Mr. Chaffanbrass did not understand all this', because 'at the Old Bailey they don't mind that kind of thing' (I, 346);[18] nevertheless, however much it means 'soiling his hands by dirty work' (I, 385), he knuckles under and sees Aram engaged. In the end, Furnival's zeal is considerably dampened: 'The skill of a lawyer he would still give if necessary, but the ardour of the loving friend was waxing colder from day to day' (II, 224).

This tangle of skill and ardour, social, professional and amatory relationship pursued through nuances of union, tension and equivocation shows Trollope at his best. This part of his study of lawyers' ethics is astute because better informed, and because he is here dealing with an intricate personality rather than an abstract popular prejudice. His technique of suggestion, showing surface behaviour controlled by barely admitted urges, is also complex and admirable. And the pairing of Lady Mason and Furnival is an effective piece of patterning, both of them motivated by the unmentionable. His technique of setting surface off against sub-surface perhaps accounts for some of the uneasiness critics have felt about his portrayal of Lady Mason and the degree of his sympathy for her.[19]

Trollope himself felt rather proud of the pathos with which he portrayed Lady Mason. 'There was nothing in [*Phineas Finn*]', he says, 'to touch the heart like the abasement of Lady Mason when confessing her guilt to her old lover' (*AA*, 321). He has the same passage in mind when, in discussing sensation novels in *An Autobiography*, he says, 'Let an author so tell his tale as to touch his reader's heart and draw his tears, and he has, so far, done his work well' (229). And yet one may find the theatrical conventionality of Lady Mason's writhing repentance rather hard to swallow. Trollope has received much less recognition for the comedy of *Orley Farm*. The first interview between Lady Mason and Mr Furnival, however, is difficult to present in solemn terms if one pays attention to the unspoken suggestion that runs through it rather than simply to the surface dialogue. Trollope's tricks of recurrence (the hands and tears) and deflection (the dashes and hesitations: ' – as a daughter') show that the comedy is intentional. That is not to say that it is simple.

What is especially interesting about Lady Mason, and mostly in her relationship with Mr Furnival, is the evidence of motives that she cannot or will not acknowledge. As the satyr is imperfectly submerged in Mr Furnival, so is the serpent in Lady Mason:

Lady Mason was rich with female charms, and she used them partly with the innocence of the dove, but partly also

with the wisdom of the serpent. . . . I do not think that she
can be regarded as very culpable. . . . She did wish to bind
these men to her by a strong attachment; but she would
have stayed this feeling at a certain point *had it been possible
for her so to manage it.*   (I, 348–9, my italics)

Trollope's comments on pathos, virtue and sympathy deflect
our attention, perhaps, from something significant that he is
doing with Lady Mason's sexuality. In an excellent essay on
'Browning and Victorian Poetry of Sexual Love', Isobel
Armstrong identifies a recurrent pattern in Victorian poetry
about women:

> the myth of the pure woman is a strangely ambiguous thing.
> If you accept it you struggle with contradictions, for an
> impossible female docility can only be given ultimate
> credence when it is seen as the product of artfulness or
> duplicity. Hence even in the most ingenuous of Victorian
> poets, such as Patmore, the pure woman is contemplated
> with an odd mixture of adulation and anger. From poet to
> poet the same pattern – docility, duplicity, anger – the same
> configuration of feeling, is struggled with, with varying
> kinds of self-consciousness and insight.[20]

Applying this scheme to Lady Mason requires some adjust-
ments, of course. She is, as Trollope insists, guilty. But a great
deal of time is spent on mitigating her sin and showing her
repentance. At the start of the novel she 'seems' to be far
removed from the follies of love-making. And in the passage
recently quoted we come closer still to Isobel Armstrong's
stereotype: 'the innocence of the dove . . . with the wisdom of
the serpent', and the reflection that she would have put limits
on her seductiveness 'had it been possible for her so to manage
it'. Though it is possible to concentrate on Lady Mason's story
as moral homily, her dealings with Mr Furnival reveal a
consistent and determined sexual cunning. The incongruity
of the manifest cunning with the pathetic surface make for
complex comedy which if not quite angry is not quite charitable either. We are not allowed to forget that Furnival is a
swain whose 'hair was grizzled and his nose was blue', nor can

we forget that Lady Mason's softness of tone and ripeness of touch are used to conceal a crime.

Lady Mason's pathos is the most effective part of her artillery, what makes her 'very comely in the eyes of the lawyer' (I, 251). 'She was a woman to know in her deep sorrow rather than in her joy and happiness; one with whom one would love to weep rather than to rejoice' (I, 260–1). Furnival (and Trollope, one supposes) is charmed by this rather sickly sex-appeal, as when he sees her at Sir Peregrine's: 'She was pale and her limbs quivered, and that look of agony, which now so often marked her face, was settled on her brow. . . . Mr. Furnival, when he looked at her, was startled by the pallor of her face, but nevertheless he thought that she had never looked so beautiful' (I, 260). On the railway back to London, he still muses on 'her pale face' and her tears (I, 264). At her second interview in Furnival's chambers, her dress is even 'blacker and more sombre than usual', her face pale and agonised; indeed 'He had never seen her look so pale, – but he said to himself at the same time that he had never seen her look so beautiful' (II, 7). And the narrator too observes, 'there was that in her figure, step, and gait of going which compelled men to turn round and look at her' (II, 6). Her 'air of feminine dependence, a proneness to lean and almost to cling as she leaned . . . might have been felt as irresistable by any man' (I, 260). Well, there is a good deal of morbid mawkishness in the taste to which Lady Mason appeals, and while Trollope suggests she is not very culpable, her management of Furnival is a clear enough indication of cunning.

At the conclusion of her first interview with him we saw her, in her helpless femininity, dropping a suggestion of bribery in his ear, a suggestion he acts upon, sending his clerk, Mr Crabwitz, in disguise to sound out the possibility of buying Dockwrath off for a thousand pounds. When she finds out that Dockwrath and Mason are indeed going to begin proceedings against her, she sits alone for hours 'planning how she would tell her story to Sir Peregrine; and again as to her second story for Mr. Furnival' (I, 150). Her second interview in Furnival's chambers, however, is occasioned by Sir Peregrine's proposal of marriage. The two Lady Masons, dove and serpent, again hold a committee meeting to think over the consequences:

how would Mr. Furnival bear it . . . ? The lawyer's knowledge, experience, and skill were as necessary to her as the
baronet's position and character. But why should Mr.
Furnival be offended by such a marriage? 'She did not
know,' she said to herself. 'She could not see that there
should be cause of offence.' But yet some inner whisper of
her conscience told her that there would be offence.   (I,
358)

Her inner whisper is quite right. The news sprung on Furnival makes him bitter and jealous, although, says Trollope, 'He
had formed no idea that the woman would become his mis-
tress' (I, 405). His disaffection would, of course, endanger her
cause, so she writes a letter of explanation, a marvel of sailing
near the wind, and asks for an appointment to see him. Let us
take one paragraph:

> When he sent for me into his library and told me what he
> wished, I could not refuse him anything. I promised obedi-
> ence to him as though I were a child; and in this way I found
> myself engaged to be his wife. When he told me that he
> would have it so, how could I refuse him, knowing as I do all
> that he has done for me, and thinking of it as I do every
> minute? As for loving him, of course I love him. Who that
> knows him does not love him? He is made to be loved. No
> one is so good and so noble as he. But of love of that sort I
> had never dreamed. Ah me, no! – a woman burdened as I
> am does not think of love.   (II, 3)

'I promised obedience to him as though I were a child' (just
obeying orders and innocent as a tender young baby). 'I found
myself engaged' (a passive and helpless bystander). 'How
could I refuse him . . . ?' (humble me, I know my place). 'Of
course I love him' (a stroke of bravado there, but then) 'Who
does not love him?' (nothing to upset yourself about). 'But of
love of that sort I had never dreamed' (I cannot even put a
name to it. 'Ah me, no!'). And yet this is a pretty forty-year-old
widow writing. Even Trollope's comment on the letter is
hesitant while sounding firm: 'There was hardly a word, – I
believe not a word in that letter that was not true' (II, 4). Which
word is giving him doubts? It sounds rather as if the narrator

is reluctant to draw the conclusions his own account of Lady Mason's manipulations would support. It may be, as Trollope says, that 'she was not willing to give up either friend, and her great anxiety was so to turn her conduct that she might keep them both' (II, 4), but if we consider this, we must reflect that the basis of all this friendship is the use she can make of it. Moreover, despite the awesome sexual power she brings to bear on these aged suitors, it is hard to believe Trollope did not mean every word when he told us that the love-making propensity of women is absent from Lady Mason, not because she is a 'pure' woman, but because her sexuality is a cunningly deployed weapon.

Allowing for that qualification, this second conference in Furnival's chambers is essentially a lovers' interview; that is, it deals with the personal feelings of lawyer and client rather than, to any significant extent, with the ordinary management of the case – with the important exception, however, that Furnival will quit in jealous pique if she marries Sir Peregrine. 'But', she says, 'I do not wish to marry him. . . . I have resolved to tell him so. That was what I said in my letter' (II, 8). Quite so, that has already been taken care of in the letter we have just looked at. Business is not the point of the interview, managing Furnival is. As compared with the first interview, this scene reaches a note of hysteria in the intensification of Lady Mason's techniques. It is conducted in superlatives. Not only is her dress blacker than black, and her face paler than ever, but she looks at him 'with eyes which would almost have melted his wife'. One cannot go farther than that. She allows Furnival the sop of thinking, as he says, 'this engagement was forced upon you' (II, 7). And her exclamation, 'My boy!' uttered almost with a shriek and followed by her bosom's 'heaving as though her heart would burst with the violence of her sobbing', gives Furnival a clue to her maternal motivation (II, 8). She concludes with a question that might already have occurred to a cooler barrister than Furnival, 'indeed, why should I take up your time further?' (II, 10).[21]

The sexual pressure of the scenes between Lady Mason and Mr Furnival is unmistakable, dramatically engaging, and psychologically convincing. As narrator, however, Trollope is very cagey about it, pooh-poohing it, while not quite denying it, as when he tells us that Mrs Furnival's jealousy:

had no ground whatever. Lady Mason may have had her faults, but a propensity to rob Mrs. Furnival of her husband's affections had not hitherto been one of them. Mr. Furnival was a clever lawyer, and she had great need of his assistance; therefore she had come to his chambers, and therefore she had placed her hand in his. That Mr. Furnival liked his client because she was good looking may be true. I like my horse, my picture, the view from my study window for the same reason. I am inclined to think that there was nothing more in it than that.   (I, 123−4)

The reader who does not catch the tempering force of that 'inclined to think' may wonder whether he and the narrator are responding to the same story. So with several assurances that neither Furnival nor Lady Mason are conscious of the sexual game they are playing. One feels that Trollope here is, as he so often says of his characters, 'teaching himself to believe'. The evident disparity between the narrator's judgements and the characters' behaviour suggests some difficulty on Trollope's part,[22] perhaps reluctant sympathy evoked by a sense of life that will not be contained comfortably within the margins of his overt moral attitudes. It may have something to do with a combination of repulsion and attraction for the notion of woman as dove and serpent that Isobel Armstrong notices in Victorian literature. And it may be inspired by the disturbing feeling about aging that recurs in Trollope's works. 'The body dries up and withers away, and the bones grow old; the brain, too, becomes decrepit, as do the sight, the hearing, and the soul. But the heart that is tender once remains tender to the last' (I, 265). This touching passage applies to Furnival, but in the context it is rhetorically distanced from him just far enough that we need not reflect on the tenderness being also adulterous. A similar note of wistfulness is struck with Sir Peregrine, but sadder, more elegiac: 'There is no Medea's caldron from which our limbs can come out young and fresh; and it were well that the heart should grow old as does the body' (II, 398).

To conclude: however misguided was Trollope's satirical view of the ethics of advocacy, his knowledge of the etiquette governing relationships between barrister, solicitor and client was sound enough. This part of his treatment of the law has a solidity and truth about it that considerably outstrips his general disgruntlement with law and lawyers in *Orley Farm*. Mr Furnival's readiness to treat Lady Mason as his client (despite his principle not to 'see people themselves') alerts the reader to something peculiar. Watching the exchanges between them carefully, the reader is treated to a display of sexual manipulation and psychology that is the more interesting in that it seems to stretch the powers of the narrator to deal with it objectively. The tension between conscious and unconscious motivation, and the narrator's note of hesitation in dealing with it, suggest an ambivalence in Trollope himself towards Lady Mason, and is related to a recurrent sexual anxiety in his novels about reaching the upper limits of middle age. Ah, me!

3 Mr Chaffanbrass for the Defence: Trollope and the Old Bailey Tradition

Mr Chaffanbrass, Trollope's most famous barrister, is identified with the Old Bailey, the very 'cock of this dunghill'. He is, says Trollope:

> a little man, and a very dirty little man. He has all manner of nasty tricks about him, which make him a disagreeable neighbour to barristers sitting near to him. He is profuse with snuff, and very generous with his handkerchief. He is always at work upon his teeth, which do not do much credit to his industry. His wig is never at ease upon his head, but is poked about by him, sometimes over one ear, sometimes over the other, now on the back of his head, and then on his nose; and it is impossible to say in which guise he looks most cruel, most sharp, and most intolerable. His linen is never clean, his hands never washed, and his clothes apparently never new. (*TC*, 482)

Adding a gratuitous racial slur, Trollope says Chaffanbrass looks more like 'a dirty old Jew' (*OF*, II, 129) than the solicitor he is untroubled to associate with, Mr Solomon Aram. Felix Graham, the fastidious young barrister of *Orley Farm*, is horrified at the prospect of assisting Chaffanbrass, 'as though he had been asked to league himself with all that was most disgraceful in the profession; – as indeed perhaps he had been' (II, 73). And Lord Fawn, in *Phineas Redux*, is appalled to find himself 'in the clutches of the odious, dirty, little man, hating the little man, despising him because he was dirty, and nothing better than an Old Bailey barrister, – and yet fearing him with so intense a fear!' (II, 236–7). Prosecutors and

50

witnesses alike cringe from the bite of 'his forensic flail', his 'impudent sarcasm and offensive sneers' (*TC*, 479–80). 'I do not think', says Trollope in *An Autobiography*, 'that I have cause to be ashamed of him' (111).

Mr Chaffanbrass appears first in *The Three Clerks* (1858) defending Alaric Tudor on a charge of embezzlement. Though the case is hopeless, Chaffanbrass effectively demolishes the Satanic Undy Scott, who has tempted Alaric to destruction. In *Orley Farm* (1862) Chaffanbrass reappears as one of a team of lawyers defending Lady Mason on a charge of perjury, after she has held an estate for twenty years on the strength of a forged will. This time we see him in association with his colleagues, such as the solicitor, Solomon Aram, and the youthfully righteous Felix Graham, assisting Chaffanbrass in the defence but deploring what he takes to be Chaffanbrass's lack of scruple (Chaffanbrass does not think much of him either). He appears finally in *Phineas Redux* (1874) defending Phineas, who has been charged with murder. He loses the first case, and wins the second though Lady Mason is guilty. In the third, the jury is instructed to acquit. An incisively drawn character, he displays Trollope's fascination with a notorious type of contemporary lawyer. Initially Trollope's depiction of him is full of prejudice about lawyers in general and criminal advocates in particular, but the three appearances mark significant stages in Trollope's appreciation of lawyers and the law. The antithetical impulses that go into Chaffanbrass's evolution, as admiration for the cleverly delineated character deepens into respect for the man behind the mannerisms, make him one of Trollope's most intriguing creations. Though he is certainly strong and sufficient in himself, we can perhaps appreciate him most fully, and understand both what Trollope is drawing upon and what contemporaries would have recognised in Chaffanbrass by seeing him in his particular social and historical context as a tough representative of a tough class.

Trollope describes Chaffanbrass as 'one of an order of barristers by no means yet extinct' (*TC*, 479). He might be a palaeozoic remnant, one who grew up with the sabre-tooth tiger (Trollope compares him to an Irish assassin [*OF*, II, 359]). But in fact, the order of barristers to which Chaffanbrass belongs was by no means very old. Chaffanbrass is not only a member of the Criminal Bar, and thus a denizen of the Old Bailey (or Central Criminal Court, as it was officially called after 1834), but a specialist in defence (as Trollope caustically puts it, a 'great guardian of the innocence – or rather not-guiltiness of the public' [*OF*, I, 342]). Before 1836, however, though counsel for those charged with treason or with misdemeanour were allowed to address the jury, counsel for those charged with a felony were not (though the custom had grown of allowing cross-examination and other services so that the deprivation of counsel in a felony case was less severely felt than it might have been). In theory, the judge was supposed to watch out for the prisoner's interests. With the Trials for Felony Act of 1836, which specified that a prisoner charged with felony had the right to 'make full answer and defence thereto by counsel learned in the law',[1] the Old Bailey defence lawyer such as Chaffanbrass, having a right not only to examine witnesses but address the jury (to 'perplex a witness and bamboozle a jury', as Trollope would have it [*TC*, 481]), came into being. His importance was the greater in that not until 1898 was a prisoner given what J. H. Baker calls 'the dangerous privilege' to be called as a witness to give sworn evidence himself, rather than through counsel, during a trial.[2] Trollope, however, sees in the Old Bailey counsel such as Chaffanbrass a special talent for 'dressing in the fair robe of innocence the foulest, filthiest wretch of his day' (*TC*, 482), and that is why Trollope, especially the early Trollope, would like to see such barristers already on the road to extinction. Chaffanbrass, then, at least in the full exercise of his powers, is a relatively new type of lawyer. Moreover, he is an especially marked example, for though barristers take what comes, prosecution or defence, we must assume Chaffanbrass to be so much in demand that he can afford to follow his own preference by choosing only defence.

When Trollope speaks of Chaffanbrass as 'nothing better than an Old Bailey barrister', he is exploiting a recognisable historical type, a type we can recover in the memoirs of several of the leading Old Bailey barristers: Serjeant Ballantine's *Some Experiences of a Barrister's Life* (1882); Montagu Williams's *Leaves of a Life* (1893); Sir Henry Hawkins's *Reminiscences of Sir Henry Hawkins* (1904); and John Witt's *Life in the Law* (1906). Hawkins, called to the Bar in 1843, described the Old Bailey as 'a den of infamy in those days not conceivable now. . . . Its associations were enough to strike a chill of horror into you. It was the very cesspool for the scourings of humanity.'³ Serjeant Ballantine recalls it was 'a term of opprobrium to be called an Old Bailey barrister'.⁴ Even the organisation of the Old Bailey was peculiar. Since it had special jurisdiction in the City of London, and London cherished its ancient independent privileges, the Old Bailey included among its judges (though usually passively), the Lord Mayor as first commissioner, with the right to 'try, hear and determine all offences', and the City Aldermen.⁵ And the court was policed by the City Constabulary rather than the Metropolitan Police. To Ballantine's mind, 'the Crown courts ought to be presided over by men who can command and enforce respect', whereas the City administrators of the court and their rituals were 'tawdry and useless monuments of a past age', and, he says, 'The mode by which officers called upon to perform high judicial duties are elected is a scandal to the age.'⁶

As ceremonial pomp, in Ballantine's view, conflicted with the efficient administration of justice at the Old Bailey, so indecent levity and callousness tarnished its solemnity. The *Quarterly Review* (1836), Williams, Ballantine, Hawkins and Theodore Hook, in his novel *Gilbert Gurney*, all deplore the indecorous feasts given for officers of the court and their guests on Mondays and Wednesdays at three and again at five o'clock during sessions. Bernard O'Donnell notes that in 1807–8 in three sessions (nineteen days) 145 dozen bottles of wine were consumed.⁷ The court chaplain, 'a stout sensual-looking man', says Williams, 'who seemed as though he were literally saturated with City feasts,' and who seldom missed both dinners, comes in for repeated mention as interrupting his dinner only to pronounce a flushed 'Amen' to the terrible sentence of death then hurrying back to his mirth, his wine and his beefsteak.⁸ In *Gilbert Gurney*, an under-sheriff, chatting cheerfully to Gilbert at one of these dinners, observes that as he has heard the sentence, he might like to witness the execution: 'We hang at eight, and breakfast at nine.'⁹ Hawkins noted the speed of after-dinner trials when judge and counsel were thus 'exhilarated': 'it may be taken', he says, 'that these after-dinner trials did not occupy on the average more than four minutes each.'¹⁰ (When Chaffanbrass gets gloomy about

the modern judge's power to influence juries by having the
last word, and says 'it usedn't to be so' [*OF*, II, 218], he may be
remembering that in the old days the judge was not even
required to sum up.[11]) Reflecting on those scenes, Ballantine
concludes: 'one cannot but look back with a feeling of disgust
to the mode in which eating and drinking, transporting and
hanging, were shuffled together.'[12]

   Though such associations and scandals clouded the general
reputation of Old Bailey barristers, two particular features of
their notoriety come closer to Chaffanbrass: their low standard of legal knowledge and their brutality in cross-
examination. To the newspaper reader, the renowned
bullying indulged in by the barristers of the Old Bailey ('Mr.
Chaffanbrass bullies when it is quite unnecessary that he
should bully; it is a labour of love' [*TC*, 481]) was part of their
gladiatorial splendour, and their notoriety evidence of their
greatness. The public 'do not understand, and so do not read
the reports of civil causes,' says Witt. 'Their idols are the
shining lights of the Central Criminal Court.'[13] Despite all this
panache, however, professionals then as now rated the learning of the criminal advocates in general very low.[14] Few judges
came from the Criminal Bar. Thus it is appropriate that
Trollope should tell us: 'As a lawyer, in the broad and high
sense of the word, it may be presumed that Mr. Chaffanbrass
knows little or nothing' (*TC*, 481). In *Orley Farm* Mr Chaffanbrass reflects, 'my chances of life have been such that they
haven't made me fit to be a judge' (II, 218). And even after he
has become a QC in *Phineas Redux*, Chaffanbrass ruminates:
'People think that the special branch of the profession into
which I have chanced to fall is a very low one, – and I do not
know whether, if the world were before me again, I would
allow myself to drift into an exclusive practice in criminal
courts' (II, 220).

   The Central Criminal Court, however, not the Courts of
Equity, was the proper school for cross-examination. There,
says Hawkins, 'presided over by a judge who knows his work,
the rules of evidence are strictly observed, and you will learn
more in six months of practical advocacy than in ten years
elsewhere.'[15] Trollope, nevertheless, took an unappreciative
view of cross-examination, seeing in it the ferocious, insolent
and systematic humiliation of witnesses. Chaffanbrass shines

at it. In *Orley Farm* he makes the witness Kenneby, who 'had
struggled hard to tell the truth, and in doing so had simply
proved himself to be an ass', despise himself and conclude 'I
aint fit to live with anybody else but myself' (II, 375). At the
other end of the social scale, Chaffanbrass reduces Lord Fawn
to mental rubble: 'his mind gave way; – and he disappeared
(*PR*, II, 432). Early in his career, as I have suggested, and with
a measure of Carlylean cocksureness, Trollope seems to have
chosen one side in a centuries-old and highly-stylised dispute
about the ethics of advocacy and the adversary system. In *The
New Zealander* (Trollope's social survey written in 1850 but
unpublished until 1972), where Trollope tried out Carlyle's
pontificating manner, Mr Allwinde's sins take on awesome
proportions. Trollope shows Allwinde's courtroom bullying,
chicanery and obfuscation, proceeds to make him representative not just of the Old Bailey but of the whole legal profession, and then argues darkly that the legal profession runs the
whole country: 'The highest officer of the Crown must be a
member of it, and as such is ranked as the second subject in the
land.' Among those who live by their work, 'it is by the bar, and
almost by the bar only' that men can enter the House of
Commons. 'The House of Lords is recruited from its members with new blood and new ability. . . . It edits newspapers,
thunders forth leading articles, and guides the world' (62).
That is coming it pretty strong – Mr Allwinde and scruffy Mr
Chaffanbrass guiding the world. And though Trollope's
understanding of and respect for Chaffanbrass's art increases
from novel to novel, cross-examination remains his King
Charles's head. As late as 1877, J. M. Langford, Blackwood's
London manager, writes of a recent dinner attended by
Trollope and Sir Henry James, who was a distinguished
criminal advocate and who became Solicitor and Attorney-
General and an intimate friend of Trollope's. There was a
great scene', says Langford, 'between Trollope and James.
Trollope raging and roaring with immense vehemence
against the system of cross-examination as practised, and
James defending it with charming calmness and good
nature.'[16]

No doubt there was some justification for Trollope's hostile
view of cross-examination. Old Bailey advocates had a reputation for insolent ferocity in the nineteenth century, though

judges gradually imposed decorum with authority the more impressive for being quietly stated. Ballantine quotes Mr Baron Alderson rebuking a reckless counsel: 'Mr ——, you seem to think that the art of cross-examination is to examine crossly.'[17] And Witt tells of Mr Justice Maule effectively dealing with a ferocious counsel and a clammed-up elderly witness: '"I really cannot answer," said the trembling lady. "Why not, ma'am?" asked the judge. "Because, my lord, he frightens me so." "So he does me, ma'am," said the judge.'[18] Whatever he thinks of advocates, Trollope has a respectful view of judges and knows the power of judicial restraint. Chaffanbrass is chastised both in *The Three Clerks* and in *Phineas Redux*. Allwinde's sarcasm in *The Macdermots of Bally-cloran* and his exhortation to an inoffensive witness to 'Go down, thou false Lothario. Go down, thou amorous Turk' (520), or Chaffanbrass's to the befuddled accountant in *The Three Clerks*, 'Go down, sir, and hide your ignominy' (484) might seem appropriate provocations for such restraint, but judges are not immune to insensibility.[19] What, other than popular prejudice, originally made Trollope so vehement about the ruthlessness of advocates is hard to say. Perhaps he inherited the Chancery lawyer's view of criminal advocates from his father, a view roundly and concisely stated by Vice-Chancellor Megarry, who asserts that Chancery lawyers are 'better than common lawyers – and no damned nonsense about "other things being equal"'.[20]

One direct experience reinforcing Trollope's stereotypical view of cross-examination and contributing clearly to one of his trial scenes is traceable to 1849. Money had disappeared from mail going through Tralee. With zeal worthy of Sherlock Holmes, Trollope, as Assistant Post-Office Surveyor, marked a coin, mailed it in a fictitious letter from a father in Newcastle to a daughter in Ardfert, and followed it. When it vanished at Tralee, Trollope, with a constable and a search-warrant, demanded that the postmaster and his assistant empty pocket and purse and found the coin in the purse of Mary O'Reilly, the assistant. Accounts of what happened vary in books on Trollope, so I shall quote parts of the trial from the *Tralee Chronicle* (31 March 1849) and the *Kerry Evening Post* (28 July 1849).[21] Actually there were two trials. The first ended without a verdict when one of the jurors fell ill and a doctor approved his release (in *The Three Clerks* Trollope notes sarcastically that 'when extremities are nigh at hand, the dying jurymen, with medical certificates, are allowed to be carried off' [502]). In this trial, Mr Brereton had the first crack at Trollope, beginning impudently:

> 'Why, Mr. Trollope, your very name is suggestive of fiction . . . Are you a son of the great witch?'[22]
> 'No . . . I am the son of Mrs. Trollope.'
> 'The novel writer?'
> 'Yes.'
> 'Have you dabbled in novels yourself?'
> 'Yes.'
> 'You drew this plan from the same source?'
> 'I did.'

In the second trial the cross-examination was higher powered. According to Justin McCarthy, who was there as a reporter, Miss O'Reilly was a pretty and popular girl, so her friends had arranged for Sir Isaac Butt, a distinguished advocate and proponent of Home Rule, to appear on her behalf. After some preliminary questions, Butt sarcastic, Trollope unruffled, about Trollope's marking of the coin, Butt then returned to the fictitious letter and Trollope as a writer of fictions, attempting as McCarthy says 'to prejudice the jury against him as a cockney slanderer who was endeavouring to cast ridicule on the institutions of the Green Isle.'[23]

Mr. Butt:	You seem to deal in fictitious characters?
Mr. Trollope:	In another way.
Mr. Butt:	Do you know 'The Macdermots of Ballycloran'?
	(laughter)
Mr. Trollope:	I know a book of that name.
Mr. Butt:	Do you remember a barrister of the name of Allwinde *(laughter)*?
Mr. Trollope:	I do.
Mr. Butt:	And another name[d] O'Napper.[24]
Mr. Trollope:	Yes.
Mr. Butt:	I believe in drawing that character, it was

	your intention to favour the world with the beau ideal of a good cross-examiner?
Mr. Trollope:	Yes. I dreamed of you (*loud laughter*).
Mr. Butt:	Do you remember the red moreen over the judge's head (*laughter*)?[25]
Mr. Trollope:	Undoubtedly.
Mr. Butt:	(reading from Mr. Trollope's book) – You thought that red moreen, if it could only speak, if it had a tongue to tell, what an indifferent account it could give of the conscience of judges, and the veracity of lawyers (*loud laughter*)? I hope you do not think that now (*laughter*)?
Mr. Trollope:	I'm rather strengthened in my opinion (*tremendous laughter*).
Mr. Butt:	[still quoting *The Macdermots*] – 'He told them what he had to say should be very brief, and considering a lawyer and a barrister, he kept his word with tolerable fidelity' (*loud laughter*). You pictured to yourself a model cross-examiner?
Mr. Trollope:	I dreamed of someone like you in cross-examination. . . .
Mr. Butt:	Fine imagination.
Mr. Trollope:	Admirable cross-examiner.

The jury retired, were locked up, deliberated all the next day, could not reach a verdict, and were discharged. Though Trollope had clearly carried off the exchange in high style, it still rankled twenty years later when Mr Chaffanbrass cross-examined 'old Bouncer, the man who writes, you know' (II, 226), in *Phineas Redux*:

'What sort of books, Mr. Bouncer?'
'I write novels,' said Mr. Bouncer, feeling that Mr. Chaffanbrass must have been ignorant indeed of the polite literature of the day to make such a question necessary.
'You mean fiction.'
'Well, yes; fiction, – if you like that word better.'
'I don't like either, particularly. . . .' (II, 230–1)

But if the memory rankled, Trollope also had the grace to be amused at his own tendency to vehemence, as suggested by the name Bouncer, and at his own deflation as Bouncer tries to reply with dignity – 'Now there was no peculiarity in a witness to which Mr. Chaffanbrass was so much opposed as an assumption of dignity' (II, 231). Chaffanbrass gets Bouncer to admit he would not even in fiction so violate probability as to have a murderer contrive and execute a murder in fifteen minutes as Phineas is supposed to have done, and ironically thanks the Attorney General for having given them the advantage of Mr Bouncer's evidence.

Fundamentally, however, it seems to me that Trollope's exasperation with cross-examination comes from a collision between one of his bedrock assumptions – that truth, by and large, is plain and available to the right-minded – and his notion of what lawyers do. He puts the issue clearly in *Orley Farm* apropos of the lawyers on both sides:

> These were five lawyers concerned, not one of whom gave to the course of justice credit that it would ascertain the truth, *and not one of whom wished that the truth should be ascertained.* Surely had they been honest-minded in their profession they would all have so wished. . . . I cannot understand how any gentleman can be willing to use his intellect for the propagation of untruth.   (II, 165, my italics)

Orley Farm is a litany of such comments. The noble Sir Peregrine asks 'what is the purport of these courts of law if it be not to discover the truth, and make it plain to the light of day?' 'Poor Sir Peregrine!' says Trollope (II, 161). Felix Graham, who spends his time in a debilitating state of moral anxiety about the law, advises, 'Let every lawyer go into court with a mind resolved to make conspicuous to the light of day that which seems to him to be the truth' (I, 179). And while Chaffanbrass fidgets, waiting for his opponent to have done, Graham worries intently over 'the absolute truth in this affair' (II, 282). But, says Trollope, 'no amount of eloquence will make an English lawyer think that loyalty to truth should come before loyalty to his client' (I, 165). His moral exasperation and impatience with the whole courtroom ritual (a different matter from his keen interest in it as drama) emerges

repeatedly, as when he says of Allwinde's attempts to bamboozle the jury in *The New Zealander*: 'Nobody who has heard
the case has the smallest doubt on the matter' (60). In short,
Trollope assumes that the truth of a client's guilt or innocence
is clear to a lawyer, or ought to be, and that a scrupulous
advocate, knowing a man guilty (Trollope does not discriminate finely between knowledge and suspicion), should refuse
his case. Even his amiable Judge Staveley subscribes to this
fastidious principle. If the lawyer believes his client innocent
he should say so roundly – Trollope seems unaware, and
would probably be annoyed to find out, that such pronounce-
ments are not allowed from counsel. Cross-examination is
bamboozling rigmarole, and the one thing needful is a flash of
Carlylean inner light to set all in order according to the merits
of the case and absolute truth.[26] Vice-Chancellor Megarry, in
Lawyer and Litigant in England, points out the shortcomings of
trying cases 'on their merits'. The decisions may rest on moral
biases not evident in the legal issues and as variable as the
personalities involved from case to case. 'Perfect justice', he
says, 'would demand an inquisition into the whole life and
behaviour of each party that would leave each crippled finan-
cially and the court exhausted. Perfect law would rigorously
exclude all save the subject matter of the suit. . . . The danger
of yearning after the merits in a court of law is that what
emerges tends to be neither true law nor true justice.'[27] The
problem of achieving total insight into a character is no
problem for Trollope since, like God, he is the creator. He
does not, at least in this early stage, consider that in life no
such total insight is available.

Trollope tells us that Mr Chaffanbrass 'was always true to
the man whose money he had taken', a point he has in
common with the Irish assassin (*OF*, II, 359). The notion that a
counsel is a hireling totally devoted to his client's cause was
usually attributed to Lord Brougham, who said, in his defence
of Queen Caroline, that 'an advocate, by the sacred duty
which he owes to his client, knows in the discharge of that
office but one person in the world, that client and none
other.'[28] The statement became famous, or at least notorious.
Chief Justice Cockburn (who helped Trollope with his book
on Palmerston), at a dinner in 1864 where Brougham reiterated his view, responded with a more central view: 'The arms

which an advocate wields he ought to use as a warrior, not as an assassin. He ought to uphold the interests of his client *per fas* and not *per nefas*. He ought to know how to reconcile the interests of his client with the eternal interests of truth and justice.'[29] Brougham himself explained that his much disputed comment was not 'a deliberate and well considered opinion' but, in the context, part of an understood threat to dispute the King's title if necessary.[30] Chaffanbrass's exclusive zeal for his client, made more tawdry by the mercenary emphasis, has, therefore, a precedent in the controversy of the period, but a shaky one.

Up to *Orley Farm* (1862), Chaffanbrass is a professional rogue and courtroom procedure, in Trollope's view, is pointlessly badgering and shameful. The whole profession is tainted with moral obliquity. Trollope admits that he has not seen a trial at the Old Bailey, and the reviewers of *Orley Farm*, most pointedly in the *London Review*,[31] attack his understanding of the law and lawyers not only on points of detail but on his whole attitude to advocacy. By the time Chaffanbrass reappears in *Phineas Redux* (written 1870–1, published 1873–4) much has changed.[32] Now, Trollope has a detailed knowledge of the Old Bailey setting – telling us, for example, how each class of spectator gets in, the distinguished guest or aristocrat on the bench, the foresighted commoner seated by arrangement with the Under-Sheriff, and the crowd of standees pushing in as the crush will allow, and he lets us see the trial from each of these perspectives through the eyes of Mr Monk, MP, Quintus Slide, newspaperman, and Mr Bunce, Phineas's landlord. But most importantly, Trollope treats the whole question of what a trial has to do with the establishment of guilt or innocence in a much more psychologically sophisticated way. And Mr Chaffanbrass, whose client Phineas is also a barrister, is allowed to put his experience and rationale of an advocate's duties before us more extensively and persuasively.

Already old when we first met him, Chaffanbrass has lately advanced in his profession, obviously not much aided by his courtroom manners. 'Caring little on whose toes he trod, whose papers he upset, or whom he elbowed on his road', he plunges into court in *The Three Clerks* carrying 'a huge old blue bag' (479). This tells us that in a long career Chaffanbrass has never been considered so particularly helpful to a QC leading a case as to prompt the QC to bestow a red bag on him as a mark of esteem; as Henry Cecil observes, 'there are few successful barristers who have not been given a red bag.'[33] But then, 'Mr. Chaffanbrass never cared what any one said' (*PR*, II, 210), and his professional manner is not calculated to curry favour. In *Phineas Redux*, however, he has become a Queen's Counsel himself, though Trollope's way of putting it successfully suggests Chaffanbrass's characteristic insouciance: 'quite late in life [he] had consented to take a silk gown' – as though he had never applied (II, 183).

Here, briefly, is the case. Phineas Finn, newly returned to Parliament, quarrels publicly with a fellow MP, Mr Bonteen, at their club. Some friends witness Phineas take a life-preserver (a cosh or small bludgeon) from his grey coat and make a semi-jocular gesture with it as Bonteen is walking away and just before Phineas sets off after him. Lord Fawn, also following Bonteen, sees a figure in a grey coat rush by in the same direction Bonteen has taken. Bonteen is found murdered and Phineas arrested on circumstantial evidence. The Reverend Joseph Emilius, who has a motive in that Bonteen was seeking evidence of Emilius's bigamous marriage to Lizzie Eustace, is also under suspicion. But he has the alibi that he was asleep in his lodging house and had no key to get in or out after the house had been locked for the night.

One indication of Trollope's tempered attitude to the law is that the cynical view, if one could call such spirited flurries cynical, is left to Lady Glencora, now Duchess of Omnium. In her zeal for Phineas's cause she wants some lawyers 'who are really, – really swells' to 'browbeat any judge and hoodwink any jury'. She tells Phineas's friend, Mr Low, a Chancery lawyer, 'I would give a carriage and a pair of horses to every one of the jurors' wives, if that would do any good. . . . I'd buy up the Home Secretary. It's very horrid to say so, of course, Mr. Low; and I daresay there is nothing wrong ever done in Chancery. But I know what Cabinet Ministers are' (II,152–4). And she sees him off with the advice, 'remember to have a great many lawyers, and all with new wigs; and let them all get in a great rage that anybody should suppose it possible that Mr. Finn is a murderer' (II, 157). No swells, but scruffy Chaffanbrass with his scruffy wig is what she must face. Despite her conviction that all things can be managed, how-

ever, she agrees with Trollope on the probity of judges, telling
Barrington Erle:

> 'There's nothing I wouldn't do. There's no getting hold
> of a judge, I know.'
> 'No, Duchess. The judges are stone.'
> 'Not that they are a bit better than anybody else, – only
> they like to be safe.'
> 'They do like to be safe.'   (II, 107)

Her enthusiasm is not without effect, however; as Mr
Wickerby, Phineas's solicitor, tells Madame Max, character
witnesses will include 'half the Cabinet. There will be two
dukes. . . . There will be three Secretaries of State. The
Secretary of State for the Home Department himself will be
examined. I am not quite sure that we mayn't get the Lord
Chancellor. . . . And there will be ever so many ladies' (II,
179). (The ladies are an appropriate novelistic touch, given
Phineas's affinities with women; but at common law, the
character of a defendant was in general irrelevant to his guilt
of a criminal charge.)

Mr Chaffanbrass commences operations in a way reminiscent of the old Chaffanbrass. He asks Lord Fawn, with Fawn's
solicitor, Mr Camperdown, to a meeting in Mr Wickerby's
office. Such an interview is quite irregular, and during the
trial the Attorney-General, Sir Gregory Grogram, leading for
the prosecution, accuses Chaffanbrass of having 'tampered'
with a witness and asks that no allusion to what transpired
there be allowed. Though Sir Gregory softens his terms from
'tampered' to 'indiscreetly questioned', Chaffanbrass likes
that little better. He 'bounced about in his place, tearing his
wig almost off his head, and defying everyone in the Court'
(II, 230). When the Lord Chief Justice submits he has been
indiscreet but allows the evidence, Chaffanbrass still refers
scornfully to 'fanciful rules of etiquette' (II, 244). Nevertheless
(American practice to the contrary) the rule was, and still is,
that 'counsel should not interview such witnesses [that is,
other than experts or professional authorities] before or during a trial'.[34] Mr Justice Hilbery in *The Duty and Art of Advocacy*
explains why: counsel should not see witnesses because he
may inadvertently or, if unscrupulous, designedly suggest to

the witness what his evidence should be.[35] The interview with Lord Fawn is, of course, a deliberate irregularity consistent with Chaffanbrass's defiant character and no accident on Trollope's part. A sign of his apprehensiveness, however, is that he takes pains to disarm nit-picking critics of his trial procedure in general by having Chaffanbrass observe that 'it was the speciality of this trial that everything in it was irregular' (II, 284). And Trollope does still go astray, as in having the judge sum up for four hours after the Attorney-General has agreed that the jury be instructed to acquit. This kind of disclaimer, however, a convenient safety net, clearly appealed to Trollope, since we find him putting it into regular service: thus a meeting of opposing lawyers in *Lady Anna* (1874) is said to be 'like all other proceedings in this cause, very irregular in its nature' (315).

Trollope, as we saw, was impatient with the sifting of evidence in matters about the truth of which he was perfectly confident. In *Phineas Redux* he has the skill to displace such exasperation to a client who, as other readers have observed, shares points of resemblance with Trollope himself. Phineas necessarily has an absolute conviction of his innocence, and his conviction is psychologically interesting since he becomes preoccupied with the difference between the legal formality of acquittal and public belief in his innocence. During his ordeal, 'the only friend whom he recognised as such was the friend who would freely declare a conviction of his innocence' (II, 215). Evidence is beside the point: 'What had he to do, – how could his innocence or his guilt be concerned, – with the manufacture of a paltry key by such a one as Mealyus?' (II, 263). His own attorney offends him – 'the company of Mr. Wickerby was not pleasant to him' – because he cannot get from Wickerby 'a sympathetic expression of assurance of his client's absolute freedom from all taint of guilt in the matter.' He is ready to change attorneys when, to the question, 'Do you believe in my innocence?' Wickerby gives the merely professional answer, 'Everybody is entitled to be believed innocent till he has been proved to be guilty.' Wickerby, in fact, does believe him guilty and 'entitled to his services, but to nothing more than his services' (II, 158–9). Whereas in *Orley Farm* the complaint was that the lawyers defend those they think guilty, here, the possibility is allowed that the client the lawyers think guilty may indeed be innocent. The question of zeal under such conditions remains. Like Pickwick,[36] Phineas insists on seeing his barrister, Mr Chaffanbrass, to be sure that Chaffanbrass believes in and will zealously proclaim his innocence. Desperate for human loyalty, he feels trapped in indifferent machinery.

Chaffanbrass prefers professional detachment: 'I hate seeing a client,' he says. 'He'll tell me either one of two things. He'll swear he didn't murder the man. . . . Which can have no effect upon me one way or the other; or else he'll say that he did, – which would cripple me altogether' (II, 213). Though there have been barristers (such as Sir Patrick Hastings) who refused on principle to see a client, the phenomenon is unusual.[37] As to being crippled by a confession, there are degrees.[38] But he would be crippled to the extent that he could not suggest his client was innocent (beyond the technical plea of Not Guilty, which tests the prosecution's ability to prove the charge), nor throw suspicion on anyone else. 'There's no knowing what they'll say,' says Chaffanbrass. 'A man will go on swearing by his God that he is innocent, till at last, in a moment of emotion, he breaks down, and out comes the truth. In such a case as this I do not in the least want to know the truth about the murder' (II, 213). An example, famous enough to be in Trollope's mind, was the 1840 case of Courvoisier, valet to Lord William Russell and charged with his murder, who confessed to his counsel, Charles Phillipps, during the trial. Phillipps made things awkward for the judge, Baron Parke, by asking his advice, but was told to continue, though hampered by the confession.[39] Chaffanbrass holds that truth absolute is not his business – 'what we should all wish to get at is the truth of the evidence', since 'there must always be attached some shadow of doubt' (II, 213). Though the case against Phineas is circumstantial, Chaffanbrass argues that most cases are, and cites the *cause célèbre* of William Palmer, the poisoner, tried in 1856: 'We were delighted to hang Palmer, – but we don't know that he killed Cook. . . . Now the last man to give us any useful insight into the evidence is the prisoner himself' (II, 214).

The difference between Phineas's and Chaffanbrass's views of what is possible and desirable to an advocate emerges at once:

'. . . there is one special thing that I want you to do. . . . I want you to make men believe that I am innocent of this crime.'

This was better than Mr. Chaffanbrass expected. 'I trust that we may succeed in making twelve men believe it,' said he. (II, 216)

Not to be diverted, Phineas declares: 'The one object that I shall have before me is the verdict of the public' (II, 220). Unexpectedly the interview does have an inspiring effect on Chaffanbrass: 'I have sometimes felt', he says, 'as though I would give the blood out of my veins to save a man. I never felt in that way more strongly than I do now' (II, 220).

Trollope's handling of this issue is subtle, however. The thoughtful reader may remember that the eloquence that moves Chaffanbrass comes from the same source as the eloquence that won Phineas the Tankerville election, on an issue adopted for tactical expedience and about which Phineas felt nothing at all. But Chaffanbrass has not after all been reformed: after his monumental speech for the defence, we learn that he still believes Phineas guilty, 'convinced that Lord Fawn had seen Phineas Finn in the street' (II, 250). That, however, is not the final word on the power of inner conviction. Though we are assured that, given the nature of the evidence, Chaffanbrass would win, what puts the victory out of doubt is Madame Max's ardour. As discontented about mere acquittal as Phineas, and as unhappy about Mr Wickerby's coolness ('She desired some adherent to her cause who would with affectionate zeal resolve upon washing Phineas Finn white as snow' [II, 180]), she is fired with the energy to go abroad and rout out the evidence that substantiates Emilius's guilt. So moral fervour *is* of account.

If Trollope presents a more balanced view of Mr Chaffanbrass and the legal process in *Phineas Redux*, as well as a more tolerant view of the moral issues, he also dramatises social attitudes to Phineas's guilt or innocence in an appropriately complex way. Honest and intelligent people are allowed to doubt his innocence. The Duke of Omnium, for example, says carefully: 'If he be acquitted I shall strive to think him innocent' (II, 191). And as for those who stand by Phineas with staunch and loving conviction, he tells Lady Laura: 'Had I murdered him in real truth, you would not have believed it' (II, 168) – conviction does not guarantee truth. Lord Fawn, sticking obstinately to his one fact, points up the existential dilemma: 'He was essentially a truth-speaking man, if only he knew how to speak the truth' (II, 240). A more bizarre phenomenon is the sympathetic interest that Phineas's supposed guilt inspires in the House: 'There was nothing, perhaps, more astonishing than the absence of rancour or abhorrence with which the name of Phineas was mentioned, even by those who felt most certain of his guilt' (II, 103); indeed, the Duchess considers him, at the moment, 'the most popular member of the House of Commons' (II, 154). Trollope elaborates in Lizzie Eustace the morbid psychology in operation. Though disgusted by her bigamous husband, Lizzie 'felt that the audacity of her husband in doing such a deed [as murdering Bonteen] redeemed her from some of the ignomity to which she had subjected herself by her marriage. . . . There was a dash of adventure about it which was almost gratifying' (II, 197–8). Moral conviction and certainty about the truth have become far more problematical in *Phineas Redux*.

Mr Chaffanbrass, then, undergoes an interesting and subtle evolution. He owes much to Trollope's satirical and stereotypical notion of advocates, as summed up in Mr Allwinde. He also belongs to the Old Bailey in ways Trollope's contemporaries would appreciate. In *The Three Clerks* and *Orley Farm*, he has to contend with Trollope's rather downright views about the transparency of guilt and innocence and the perverse proclivity of lawyers to moral obliquity and shady practice. *Phineas Redux*, however, shows a considerable advance in understanding, and Chaffanbrass, though he maintains his familiar irreverence, flowers with it.

All along, of course, there was another Chaffanbrass – the domestic. At home the tiger becomes a lamb, 'one of the most easy, good-tempered, amiable old gentlemen that ever was pooh-poohed by his grown-up daughters, and occasionally told to keep himself quiet in a corner' (*TC*, 483). The man who lets loose 'the wretch whose hands are reeking with the blood of father, mother, wife, and brother' also 'subscribes largely to hospitals founded for the relief of the suffering poor' (*TC*, 482–3). Horses persecute him. He arrives late in court in *The Three Clerks* because his horse has fallen down in the street, to be told with quiet awesomeness by the judge: 'My horse never falls down in the street, Mr. Chaffanbrass' (479). And in *Phineas Redux* he makes the double error of buying his daughter a horse from a gentleman, who cheats him, and consulting an attorney about it, who goes for arbitration 'with the horse eating his head off every meal at ever so much per week' (II, 212). At Phineas's trial the old man speaks for four hours, refreshes himself with 'a pint of port wine', and continues for another three: 'It was said of him afterwards that he was taken home speechless by one of his daughters and immediately put to bed, that he roused himself about eight and ate his dinner and drank a bottle of port in his bedroom, that he then slept', appearing in court the next day none the worse for wear (II, 250–1). One does not know whether to be more touched by the domestic affection or respectful of his capacity for port. His general shabbiness, over which his daughters cannot triumph, is perhaps a relic of his early career, since, despite the glamour, Old Bailey lawyers earned comparatively little: 'Barristers who practised at the Old Bailey', say Abel-Smith and Stevens, 'were generally believed to be disreputable, and the earnings for criminal work were a tenth of those for civil work.'[40] He is a success now, and the shabbiness a matter of style, the deceptively uncouth appearance of the deadly warrior, as Lord Fawn perceives.

Chaffanbrass is a fine creation, rich in historical association, impressive on his first appearance, and impressive in his evolution, despite Trollope's occasional inaccuracies.[41] What is happiest about him, perhaps, is that this evolution is the sign of an evolution in Trollope himself from indulgence in cocksure traditional satire to a large measure of sympathy and understanding, even on the score of his old bugbear, cross-examination. 'You can frighten a witness,' says Mr Wickerby. And Chaffanbrass replies: 'It's just the trick of the trade that you learn, as a girl learns the notes of her piano. There's nothing in it. You forget it all the next hour. But when a man has been hung whom you have striven to save, you do remember that' (*PR*, II, 221).

4 *Lares et Penates* – Solicitors and Estates

A pamphlet of 1680 defines a solicitor as a 'pettyfogging sophister' who differs from a lawyer 'as a shrimp does from a lobster, a frog from an elephant, and a tom-tit from an eagle'.[1] Though solicitors were originally connected with Chancery and attorneys with common law, parliamentary acts of 1729 and 1750 removed any substantial distinctions in qualification or practice. Sampson Brass of *The Old Curiosity Shop* is 'one of her Majesty's attorneys of the Courts of King's Bench and Common Pleas at Westminster and a solicitor of the High Court of Chancery', but the term 'solicitor', a 'modern new-fangled one' in the opinion of the lawyer-novelist Samuel Warren, and much to his disgust, was taking over.[2] Despite the efforts of the Society of Gentlemen Practisers, solicitors and attorneys never attained the prestige that barristers enjoyed, nor were the higher legal appointments open to them. Barristers, trained at the Inns of Court, where the students traditionally came from the nobility and gentry, claimed to be gentlemen, though by the nineteenth century that claim might rest on little more than a modest middle-class background.[3] Throughout the eighteenth century, solicitors had a low social reputation: it was claimed that tradesmen who had failed at everything else became solicitors.[4] Curious about a stranger, Dr Johnson observed that 'he did not care to speak ill of any man behind his back, but he believed the gentleman was an attorney.'[5] Changes came but the soreness remained. Harry Kirk, in his history of the solicitors' profession, notes, for example, that though 'on every count other than the Bar's monopoly of legal appointments the professional and social distinction [between barristers and solicitors] had by the mid-nineteenth century lost its justification,' nevertheless, attorneys and solicitors were 'acutely sensitive about their social

69

status and reputation'.[6] These facts may help us to appreciate
the great range in status and respectability among Trollope's
solicitors, from Soames and Simpson, who Squire Prosper
doubts are gentlemen, to Messrs Grey and Barry, who are;
from the unimpeachable probity of Slow and Bideawhile or
Camperdown and Son to 'Mowbray and Mopus; – horrible
people," says Camperdown, 'sharks, that make one blush for
one's profession' (*ED*, 100), or to Mr Squercum, 'so clever, and
so pestilential' (*WWLN*, II, 70).

It may be helpful (especially for non-English readers whose
legal system may be different) to note briefly other ways in
which solicitors differ from barristers. Solicitors may belong
to firms and have partnerships, but barristers, though they
may share chambers, are independent. Solicitors are spread
about the country, whereas barristers are concentrated in
London. Solicitors see and are hired by the public, but barristers are briefed by solicitors. Solicitors have right of audience
in inferior courts but not, in general, in the superior courts.
Solicitors give general advice to their clients on legal and
business matters, deal with the acquisition, sale and transfer of
land, draft documents such as wills, trusts and settlements,
administer trusts and probate business, take evidence from
witnesses and instruct counsel. Since they deal directly with
the public, solicitors become identified with the interests of
their clients, often over generations. And, since it is the
solicitor who sees the lay client, when an Englishman says he
will see his lawyer, he normally means his solicitor.

Among the many partnerships of solicitors in Trollope's
novels, the major firm is that of Slow and Bideawhile, who
appear in several of them.[7] They are already old when they
first appear. In *Orley Farm*, Mr Slow is 'old Slow'. In *Miss
Mackenzie*, he is 'a grey-haired old man, nearer eighty than
seventy, who . . . had attended those same chambers in
Lincoln's Inn Fields daily for the last sixty years,' and Mr
Bideawhile is 'almost as old as himself' (221). And in *The Way
We Live Now*, Slow is 'gathered to his fathers' (II, 69). Trollope
emphasises their age in order to suggest that they are of a
more honest generation. Thus when Sir Peregrine Orme in
Orley Farm suggests that Slow and Bideawhile be employed to
defend Lady Mason on a perjury charge, the successful modern barrister, Mr Furnival, has his qualms:

there were no more respectable men in the whole profession. But then Mr. Furnival feared that they were too
respectable. They might look at the matter in so straighfor-
ward a light as to fancy their client really guilty; and what
might happen then? . . . Mr. Furnival, therefore, was obliged to say that Slow and Bideawhile did not undertake that
sort of business.   (I, 263–4)

And when Furnival goes through the motions of speaking to
him, Slow does indeed refuse the case (I, 385). Trollope's
point about the deteriorating probity of the times is made
even more explicitly in *The Way We Live Now*, where the sharp
upstart, Mr Squercum, is a notable, if ungentlemanly, success:
'fairly honest, though it must be owned that among the
Bideawhiles of the profession this was not the character which
he bore.' He is 'a sign, in his way, that the old things are being
changed' (II, 70–1). So with other firms. In Round and Crook,
'Mr. Round senior had enjoyed the reputation of being a
sound, honourable man, but was now considered by some to
be not quite sharp enough for the practice of the present day'
(*OF*, I, 157–8). And in *Mr Scarborough's Family*, old Mr Grey,
contemplating the tendency of his partner, Mr Barry, to sharp
practice, concludes: 'I have been at my business long enough.
Another system has grown up which does not suit me. . . It
may be that 'I am a fool, and that my idea of honesty is a
mistake' (600). *O tempora, O mores!* And yet Trollope's recurrent sense of the relative wickedness of modern lawyers will
hardly bear examination. Just as he was wrong about Chaffanbrass being a vestige of old, bad ways, so his sense of the
vanishing probity of solicitors, if these various instances I have
been quoting amount to a general view, is unreliable. Solicitors were better trained and better disciplined as the century
proceeded. And as for the good old days, Slow, Bideawhile,
Round senior, and Grey might well reflect on those charming
companions of their youth, Dodson and Fogg.

In fact, Slow and Bideawhile, for all their probity, are not
shown to be very clever. 'The Bideawhiles piqued themselves
on the decorous and orderly transaction of their business. It
had grown to be a rule in the house that anything done quickly
must be done badly' (*WWLN*, II, 69–70). And yet, for all their
deliberation, they seem initially to have given Miss Mackenzie

her property by mistake, and later they allow her to lend a large sum of money without checking on the supposed security, which is already mortgaged elsewhere. They manage no better in the sale of the Longestaffe property in *The Way We Live Now*. Indeed, notwithstanding his feeling that social mores have disintegrated, Trollope's young lawyers, young Round or the 'mean-looking' Squercum, though not more kindly, are more astute than their elders.

Though Trollope's views about the declining decorum of solicitors may be suspect, his depiction of their base of operations, the solicitor's office, seems very accurate. Slow and Bidewhile, though successful, prestigious, and vain about their aristocratic clients, conduct their business in chambers which, in their jumbled ugliness, were apparently typical of Victorian solicitor's offices. Michael Birks, in *Gentlemen of the Law*, says, 'So far as outward show was concerned, solicitors had long since been regarded as insensible to their surroundings, and the numerous descriptions of solicitors' offices to be found in the novels of Charles Dickens are not exaggerations.'[8] The office of Slow and Bidewhile seems to conform in all respects to this standard of insensibility:

There is, I think, no sadder place in the world than the waiting-room attached to an attorney's chambers in London. In this instance it was a three-cornered room, which had got itself wedged in between the house which fronted to Lincoln's Inn Fields, and some buildings in a narrow lane that ran at the back of the row. There was no carpet in it, and hardly any need of one, as the greater part of the floor was strewed with bundles of dusty paper. There was a window in it, which looked out from the point of the further angle against the wall of the opposite building. The dreariness of this aspect had been thought to be too much for the minds of those who waited, and therefore the bottom panes had been clouded, so that there was in fact no power of looking out at all. Over the fireplace there was a table of descents and relationship, showing how heirship went; and the table was very complicated, describing not only the heirship of ordinary real and personal property, but also explaining the wonderful difficulties of gavelkind, and other mysteriously traditional laws. But the table was as dirty as it was complicated, and the ordinary waiting reader could make nothing of it. There was a small table in the room, near the window, which was always covered with loose papers; but these loose papers were on this occasion again covered with sheets of parchment, and a pale-faced man, of about thirty, whose beard had never yet attained power to do more than sprout, was sitting at the table, and poring over the parchments. Round the room, on shelves, there was a variety of iron boxes, on which were written the names of Mr. Slow's clients – of those clients whose property justified them in having special boxes of their own. . . . There was, however, one such box open, on the middle of the floor, and sundry of the parchments which had been taken from it were lying around it.   (*MM*, 217–18)

The scene is from *Miss Mackenzie*, and Trollope makes it work for him. Since there is no other space, John Ball and Margaret Mackenzie are put there to wait. Since the box and papers strew the floor, Ball's eye falls on one of them endorsed 'in almost illegible old English letters: "Jonathan Ball, to John Ball, junior – Deed of Gift"' (219). It is the lost deed, uncovered by Mr Slow, that will strip his client, Miss Mackenzie, of her fortune and give it to John Ball – Slow will be honest though it make his client a pauper. The office scene is quietly metaphorical. From the documentary rubble of experience, the dusty sediment of the past on Slow and Bidawhile's floor, a fragment surfaces to determine the shape of unsuspecting lives. The law is a regulator of human affairs, but striking out of the blue as it does in *Miss Mackenzie*, or plodding with a massive indifference that takes years to overcome as in *Lady Anna*, the law in Trollope's novels sometimes operates like George Eliot's or Hardy's destiny.

There is poetry in it too. Though the solicitor's principle occupation, conveyancing, effecting the transfer of land and dealing with the rights and titles relating to it, might seem a dry subject to the layman, Trollope, like Dickens, recognises its romance, though Dickens is more satirical. Mr Snitchey in Dickens's *The Battle of Life* monomaniacally rhapsodises:

'Here's a smiling country . . . once overrun by soldiers – trespassers every man of 'em – and laid waste by fire and sword. He, He, He! . . . But take this smiling country as it stands. Think of the laws appertaining to real property; to the bequest and devise of real property; to the mortgage and redemption of real property; to leasehold, freehold, and copyhold estate; think,' said Mr. Snitchey, with such great emotion that he actually smacked his lips, 'of the complicated laws relating to title and proof of title, with all the contradictory precedents and numerous acts of parliament connected with them; think of the infinite number of ingenious and interminable chancery suits, to which this pleasant prospect may give rise; – and acknowledge, Dr. Jeddler, that there is a green spot in the scheme about us!⁹

Trollope recognises a different sort of poetry, stemming not only from the law's labyrinthine subtleties but from the solicitor's bond with an estate and the virtually spiritual significance of landed estates themselves.

Where the barrister maintains a necessary detachment from his lay client, at the extreme refusing even to see him, the solicitor becomes identified with his client. As Megarry points out, it was even argued in 1773 that 'The connection between attorney and client is considered in law, as nearer than that between baron and feme; the former being considered only as one single person; the latter, as two souls in one flesh.'¹⁰ Trollope recognises this bond, even to the extent of calling in doubt his gloomy notion of the declining reputation of solicitors. He asks:

> Is it not remarkable that the common repute which we all give to attorneys in general is exactly opposite to that which every man gives to his own attorney in particular? Whom does anybody trust so implicitly as he trusts his own attorney? And yet is it not the case that the body of attorneys is supposed to be the most roguish body in existence? (*MM*,   222)

A firm like Slow and Bideawhile or like Camperdown and Son, looking after the interests of an estate such as that of the Eustaces generation after generation, becomes privy to its secrets and, because of the peculiar combination of detachment and involvement in the relationship, acts as a stabiliser against the passing whims and frivolities of members of the family itself. The bond is an almost mystical one. Preoccupied as Trollope is with the national spirit and tradition, the Englishness of England, as embodied in the church, in parliament, and in the law, he would fully appreciate Sir Frederick Pollock's meditation in *The Land Laws* on the quasi-religious function of the solicitor. A modern observer, writes Pollock,

> may speculate on a remote connection of Pitris and Lares with the domestic chaplain, the ancestral monuments in the parish church, or the family pew. Or, when he notes who is now the real possessor of the secrets of the estate, the real familiar spirit at whose bidding the magical powers of the settlement are called forth, and without whose aid no matter of weight can be undertaken, he may peradventure dream that 'the disestablished Lar' . . . is not dead but transformed, and lives embodied in the family solicitor.[11]

The estate itself in Trollope, for which the solicitor performs this tutelary function, is the outward and visible sign of an inward and spiritual grace.[12]

In *Ralph the Heir*, for example, the Newton estate 'carried with it a value which, in the eyes of Sir Thomas [Underwood], – and, indeed, in the eyes of all English-men, – was beyond all money price, though the territorial position was, for a legitimate heir, almost a principality' (I, 210). Even Neefit, the breeches maker, tells Ralph, 'If I'd the chance I'd sooner beg, borrow, starve, or die, before I'd sell it; – let alone working, Captain' (I, 261). Though Ralph the heir is a feckless, vapid, ne'er-do-well puppy, and his illegitimate cousin, also named Ralph, who may inherit if the reversion is bought up, is 'the trusted friend of all the tenants' (I, 129) and cares for the estate and its people, the tenants nevertheless prefer Ralph the true heir. 'It would have been more consistent with the English order of things' that the legitimate heir should inherit, says even the admirable Ralph himself (I, 337). Presenting Sir Gregory Newton's attempt to buy the reversion for his bastard son as tragic hubris, Trollope preserves the mystic order by having Sir Gregory break his neck while hunting just as the deal is about to be concluded. So the puppy inherits. 'It was in proper conformity with English habits and English

feelings that the real heir should reign' (II, 85). Trollope
agrees with Burke in seeing a spiritual congruity between the
descent of entailed property, the life of the nation, and the
idea of society. 'We receive,' says Burke, 'we hold, we transmit
our government and our privileges, in the same manner in
which we enjoy and transmit our property and our lives,' and
the perpetuation of family property 'tends the most to the
perpetuation of society itself.' As Burke sees 'each contract of
each particular state' as 'but a clause in the great primeval
contract of eternal society' holding 'all physical and all moral
natures, each in their appointed place,'[13] so Trollope sees the
estate as a similar clause in the English spiritual contract.

The solicitor, therefore, has a difficult and significant role
to play. He has the personal and transient pecuniary interests
of members of the family at heart, but also the inherited
dignity and welfare of the estate in general, and he must
exercise reason, scholarship and the law's machinery to protect both. He has to contend with the wickedness, passion, and
perversity of his clients' enemies, but also with the indifference and trickery of the very people he represents. We shall
see Mr Grey driven to distraction by the outrageous legal
ingenuity of his client, Mr Scarborough. But the most perti-
nent example of a solicitor fighting on two fronts at once to
protect an estate against both the incursions of a marauder
and the indifference of its owner is that of Mr Camperdown
and his clients, the Eustaces, in *The Eustace Diamonds*.

Some account of the situation is necessary. From childhood
Lizzie Greystock has had a magpie's love of jewels. When she
marries, she lies to her husband, Sir Florian Eustace, about
debts she already owes for jewels, and he catches her out. But
the Eustaces tend to die young, and he follows the family
pattern, whereupon, his widow being pregnant, the following
possibilities arise. If a son is born, he inherits everything. If a
daughter is born, she inherits the personal wealth, while Sir
Florian's brother, John Eustace, inherits the family's
Yorkshire estates. If no child survives, John inherits everything upon Lizzie's demise. In the meantime, as widow, she
has the Scottish property, Portray Castle, for life, though she
chooses to believe it is hers absolutely. 'For so clever a woman
she was infinitely ignorant as to the possession and value of
money and land and income' (10). Moreover, she claims that a

diamond necklace worth ten thousand pounds was given to
her outright by Sir Florian and that the diamonds are therefore hers to do with as she will. Her claim outrages Mr
Camperdown, who disliked her from the first, and he becomes
obsessed with frustrating her pig-headed greed and regaining
the diamonds, pinning his hopes on the idea that they are
heirlooms and could not be given away. Lizzie refuses to
answer his letters. He seeks advice from the learned barrister,
Thomas 'Turtle' Dove, and, despite the discouraging opinion
he gets from Dove, institutes proceedings in Chancery. At a
hotel room in Carlisle on her way to London from Scotland,
Lizzie is robbed of her jewellery box. The diamonds happen to
be under her pillow, but she makes a false declaration of
robbery, hoping that Camperdown will give up if he thinks
the diamonds lost. In London she is robbed again, this time
successfully, and, being steeped in lies, gives another false
declaration to a magistrate. Police detectives go to work, and
when the thieves are apprehended Lizzie confesses her perjury so sweetly at the police-court that the magistrate himself
is softened by her pretty state of distress. The jewels, however,
are irrecoverable. Camperdown fails in his object, and Lizzie
ends as she began, enjoying her lies, 'thinking them to be more
beautiful than truth' (719).

The Eustace Diamonds is an acerbic novel. Lizzie is 'an opulent
and aristocratic Becky Sharp' (18), and a very successful one.
She is also a cheap, stubborn and exasperating hypocrite, but
she has a maudlin, slip-slop sense of poetry that aids her in
self-justication: 'True love, true friendship, true benevolence,
true tenderness, were beautiful to her . . . and therefore she
was always shamming love and friendship and benevolence
and tenderness' (125). As a creation she is tremendously
impressive. In comparison, Mr Camperdown may seem to
hold a minor place in the novel, overshadowed by the usual
array of lovers: Frank Greystock, Lord Fawn, Lord George de
Bruce Caruthers and Mr Emilius for the men, Lizzie, Lucinda
Roanoke and Lucy Morris for the women. But Camperdown's
significance is disproportionate to the space he occupies. He is
Lizzie's major antagonist. He lays siege to her, and her actions
are largely determined by his persistence. Even her lovers
find themselves obliged to reckon with Camperdown. She
tries, for example, to recruit Lord Fawn, taking

Camperdown's letter from under her Bible to show him. But unfortunately Camperdown is also Lord Fawn's lawyer, his own guardian spirit.

> That Mr. Camperdown should be in the wrong in such a matter was an idea which never occurred to Lord Fawn. There is no form of belief stronger than that which the ordinary English gentleman has in the discretion and honesty of his own family lawyer. What his lawyer tells him to do, he does. What his lawyer tells him to sign, he signs. He buys and sells in obedience to the same direction, and feels perfectly comfortable in the possession of a guide who is responsible and all but divine. 'What diamonds are they?' asked Lord Fawn in a very low voice.   (90)

No blandishment can prevail against this trust – Lizzie is merely the woman he loves, Mr Camperdown is his lawyer. 'Every word that Mr. Camperdown said was gospel to Lord Fawn' (100). When, upon hearing Camperdown and taking his side, Lord Fawn insists that Lizzie restore the diamonds, she despises him. Taking the same limpet's attitude to him as to the diamonds, however, she determines she will marry him, thus giving him something to worry about for much of the rest of the book. Under Lizzie's charm, Frank Greystock, himself a barrister, opposes Camperdown's views and takes upon himself the role of protector of innocence – but he has the instinct not to inquire too closely into the facts, accepting Lizzie's viewpoint along with her sexual attraction.

Camperdown is the sort of solicitor Sir Frederick Pollock described as the family Lar. 'Mr. Camperdown was a gentleman of about sixty, who had been lawyer to Sir Florian's father, and whose father had been lawyer to Sir Florian's grandfather' (36). His devotion is more than a matter of long connection: 'The interests of his clients were his own interests, and the legal rights of the properties of which he had the legal charge, were as dear to him as his own blood' (251). That being understood, 'His connection with the property and with the family was of a nature to allow him to take almost any liberty with the Eustaces.' Thus upon John Eustace's adopting the complacent view that, if Lizzie persists, the heir will still have plenty of money to buy more diamonds, 'Mr.

Camperdown took upon himself to say that he'd "be —— if
he'd put up with it!"' (36). For Camperdown the interests of
the estate transcend the wishes of the temporary owners, and
it becomes a trial to him that John Eustace should be so
feckless. 'Mr. Camperdown groaned over the matter with
thorough vexation of spirit. . . . His luck in the matter was so
bad! John Eustace had no backbone, no spirit, no proper
feeling as to his own family' (249–50). Lizzie's pig-headed
avariciousness is a thing unendurable to Camperdown.

> Ten thousand pounds! It was, to Mr. Camperdown's mind,
> a thing quite terrible that, in a country which boasts of its
> laws and of the execution of its laws, such an imposter as was
> this widow should be able to lay her dirty, grasping fingers
> on so great an amount of property, and that there should be
> no means of punishing her. . . . Mr. Camperdown knew
> that the harpy was wrong – that she was a harpy, and he
> would not abandon the cause.   (249–50)

As Lizzie's tight-fisted grasp is elemental, inaccessible to
reason, Camperdown's response is instinctive, personal,
moral, less a professional concern than a divine rage.

Camperdown's great hope lies in the thought that the
Eustace diamonds are an heirloom. Sir Florian's grandfather
had stated in his will that the jewels were to be so regarded,
and Camperdown believes that, as an heirloom, the necklace
cannot be given away, and that Lizzie must therefore give it
back. Frank Greystock, sympathetic to Lizzie, thinks the same
when Lizzie tells him how Sir Florian said she was 'to regard it
as her own peculiar property. "If it was an heirloom he
couldn't do it," Frank had said, with all the confidence of a
practising barrister' (144). But Camperdown's confidence is
misplaced. 'It could not be said of him that he was a learned
lawyer' (251), says Trollope, and when Camperdown consults
the learned barrister, Mr Dove, for an opinion, the result is a
nasty surprise.

I will now summarise the learned Dove's opinion (as
written for Trollope by his friend, the barrister Charles
Merewether[14]) and the glosses on it which appear in Chapters
25 and 28. First, though many may think that any chattel may
be an heirloom, the law discriminates. An heirloom must have

a continuing and identifiable form, which a necklace, whose
setting may be altered from generation to generation, does
not have. The Crown jewels, 'representing not the possession
of the sovereign but the time-honoured dignity of the Crown',
are an exception, and the decision that they are an exception
denies the right to other jewels. Spelman, in defining an
heirloom, describes it as *'omne utensil robustius'* – thus a bed, a
table, a pot or a pan may be an heirloom, but not a necklace.
Secondly, an heirloom is not devisable, cannot be bequeathed
by a will. Heirlooms go to the heir by special custom. In all this,
says Mr Dove, the law has been concerned not with the mere
protection of property but, poetically,

> with the more picturesque idea of maintaining chivalric
> associations. Heirlooms have become so . . . that the son or
> grandson or descendent may enjoy the satisfaction which is
> derived from saying, my father or my grandfather or my
> ancestor sat in that chair, or looked as he now looks in that
> picture, or was graced by wearing on his breast that very
> ornament which you now see lying beneath the glass. . . .
> The Law, which in general, concerns itself with our property
> or lives and our liberties, has in this matter bowed gracefully
> to the spirit of chivalry and has lent its aid to romance; – but
> it certainly did not do so to enable the discordant heirs of a
> rich man to settle a simple dirty question of money, which,
> with ordinary prudence, the rich man should himself have
> settled before he died.   (256)

Small comfort to Camperdown, concerned to protect the
property. But that is not the worst of it. Dove adds that 'Pearls
and jewels, even though only worn on state occasions, may
go to the widow as paraphernalia' (225). Paraphernalia!
Camperdown 'had never as yet heard of a claim made by a
widow for paraphernalia' (251). Had he read his Blackstone
carefully, he would have been less surprised. I suspect Trollope
had; it may have suggested to him this crux in the novel.
Blackstone says:

> And, as the husband may thus, generally, acquire a property
> in all the personal substance of the wife, so in one particular
> instance the wife may acquire a property in some of her

husband's goods; which shall remain to her after his death, and shall not go to his executors. These are called her *paraphernalia*; which is a term borrowed from the civil law, and is derived from the Greek language, signifying something over and above her dower. Our law uses it to signify the apparel and ornaments of the wife, suitable to her rank and degree; which she becomes entitled to at the death of her husband over and above her jointure or dower, and preferably to all other representatives: and the jewels of a peeress, usually worn by her, have been held to be *paraphernalia*. Neither can the husband devise by his will such ornaments and jewels of his wife; though during his life perhaps he hath the power (if unkindly inclined to exert it) to sell them or give them away. But if she continues in the use of them till his death, she shall afterwards retain them against his executors and administrators, and all other persons, except creditors where there is a deficiency of assets. And her necessary apparel is protected even against the claim of creditors.[15]

In sum, the will of Sir Florian's grandfather is of no consequence in making the diamonds an heirloom since heirlooms cannot be devised. A necklace cannot be an heirloom, so it cannot be retrieved from Lizzie on that ground. Moreover, a necklace can be paraphernalia and therefore belong to the wife.

The only scrap of comfort left to Mr Camperdown is that there are certain limits to paraphernalia. The diamonds seem too expensive to be so classed, and Dove therefore doubts that Lizzie would have the power to alienate them from the estate. This is slender consolation.

'A necklace can't be an heirloom!' said Mr. Camperdown to himself, telling off on his fingers half-a-dozen instances in which he had either known or had heard that the head of a family had so arranged the future possession of the family jewels. . . . A pot or a pan might be an heirloom, but not a necklace! Mr. Camperdown could hardly bring himself to believe that this was law. And then as to paraphernalia! (251)

Camperdown's obsession is evident in the language he is inspired to apply to Lizzie: 'that greedy siren, that heartless snake, that harpy of a widow' (227). John Eustace's wishes are beside the point. A bill is filed in Chancery: 'which hostile proceeding was, in truth, effected by the unaided energy of Mr. Camperdown, although Mr. Camperdown put himself forward simply as an instrument used by the trustees of the Eustace property' (338).

Dove and Camperdown have a nicely adjusted relationship of balanced sympathies and tensions. They share a poetic and mystical notion of the law, a notion in which lawyers figure as shepherds to a wayward flock:

> they equally entertained a deep-rooted contempt for that portion of mankind who thought that property could be managed and protected without the intervention of lawyers. The outside world to them was a world of pretty, laughing, ignorant children; and lawyers were the parents, guardians, pastors and masters by whom the children should be protected from the evils incident to their childishness. (254)

Unwelcome, even outrageous, as Mr Dove's opinion is to Camperdown, he is moved by the barrister's commentary. Dove's remarks on the chivalry of the law appeal to Camperdown's moral sensibility:

> Mr. Camperdown had not unfrequently heard him speak in the same fashion before, and was accustomed to his manner of unravelling the mysteries and searching into the causes of Law with a spirit which almost lent poetry to the subject. When Mr. Dove would do so, Mr. Camperdown would not quite understand the words spoken, but he would listen to them with an undoubting reverence. And he did understand them in part, and was conscious of an infusion of a certain amount of poetic spirit into his own bosom. He would think of these speeches afterwards, and would entertain high but somewhat cloudy ideas of the beauty and the majesty of Law. Mr. Dove's speeches did Mr. Camperdown good, and helped to preserve him from that worst of all diseases, – a low idea of humanity. (256–7)

They both consider the diamonds in a moral light, but unfortunately their views are at odds. Camperdown's role as guardian prompts him to dwell on the considerable value of the diamonds and magnify their importance. Mercy is out of the question. Mr Dove, on the other hand, is morally radical: diamonds are worthless. With a touch of malice, as from a man who hankers after no baubles, he declares: 'it is, upon the whole, well for the world that property so fictitious as diamonds should be subject to the risk of such annihilation' (651). Though they may give rise to 'one or two points of interest' about rights of possession '"the very existence of such property so to be disposed of, or so not to be disposed of, is in itself an evil. Then, we have had to fight for six months about a lot of stones hardly so useful as the flags in the street. . . ." All of which Mr. Camperdown did not quite understand' (709–10).

Camperdown must pursue the matter to the end, even after the diamonds are stolen: 'the widow's liability in regard to the property was not at all the less because she had managed to lose it through her own pig-headed obstinacy' (648). He is ready to take up Mr Dove's suggestion that if ownership by the Eustace estate could be established in a Chancery suit, then restitution could be sought in a second suit at common law, but John Eustace will not have it. In fact, in the whole matter, the only thing that seems to irritate Eustace is Lizzie's cutting down the timber of the Portray estate (116) – but then, timber is special. It is a bitter end for Mr Camperdown. Refusing to testify at the robbery trial, Lizzie holes up in Scotland.

> And this was the end of the Eustace diamonds as far as anything was ever known of them in England. Mr. Camperdown altogether failed, even in his attempt to buy them back at something less than their value, and was ashamed himself to look at the figures when he found how much money he had wasted for his clients in their pursuit. (709)

Contemplating the whole structure of lies, machinations, perjury and wreckage, Frank Greystock, his eyes opened at last, concludes: 'And all this had been done for nothing, – had been done, as he thought, that Mr. Camperdown might be kept in the dark, whereas all the light in the world would have assisted Mr. Camperdown nothing' (643).

Structure, arguments, and characters are intimately bound to legal issues in *The Eustace Diamonds*. Discussion of them forms a good part of the novel's discourse, discourse enlivened by zeal, obstinacy and passion. Legal scholarship and precision provide the rules and surprises for a tense game of snakes and ladders that closely engages everyone: 'there was hardly a lawyer of repute but took up the question, . . . The Attorney and Solicitor-General were dead against her' (444–5). Lady Glencora takes up the cause, and even the Duke of Omnium waits breathlessly for the latest reports. And at the centre of things is Mr Camperdown, somewhat prosaic himself, no great scholar, glimpsing at times the poetry of the law, and serving as guardian spirit in the religion of estates.

As one speaks of nuns as the brides of the church, one might speak of Trollope's best solicitors as married to the English constitution as it works itself out in the whole articulate and inarticulate, rational and irrational, English way of doing things. In *The American Senator*, which has a great deal to say about the sacred irrationality of English institutions, the bond between solicitor and estate, if not 'nearer than that between baron and feme', is nevertheless sanctified by marriage, the marriage of the solicitor's daughter, Mary Masters, to the heir of Bragton.

> The attorney when he got to the gate stopped a moment and looked up the avenue with pardonable pride. The great calamity of his life, the stunning blow which had almost unmanned him when he was young and from which he had never quite been able to rouse himself, had been the loss of the management of the Bragton property. His grandfather and his father had been powerful at Bragton, and he had been brought up in the hope of walking in their paths. Then strangers had come in, and he had been dispossessed. But how was it with him now? It had almost made a young man of him again when Reginald Morton, stepping into his office, asked him as a favour to resume his old task. But what was that in comparison with this later triumph? His own child was to be made queen of the place! His grandson, should she be fortunate enough to be the mother of a son, would be the squire himself!   (497)

What could be more fitting?

The theology of estates and its irrational compulsions are symbolically elaborated in *The Way We Live Now*, but with a sense that the religion has entered upon an age of cynicism and disintegration. Roger Carbury, the novel's moral exemplar, living in a manor surrounded by a moat, is a figure of chivalric probity in an increasingly dishonest time. He and his estate represent embattled integrity. To none of the great houses around him 'belonged that thoroughly established look of old county position which belonged to Carbury' (I, 129). As we saw earlier, though Roger's estate is unencumbered by any entail, and though his second cousin, Felix, is 'the man whom of all others he most despised', nevertheless, 'Sir Felix was the natural heir, and this man felt himself constrained, almost as by some divine law, to see that this land went by natural descent.' He would rather the estate 'be dissipated by a Carbury than held together by a stranger' (I, 131–2). The new way of things is represented by the financier, Melmotte, who entertains the deluded assumption that he can secure to himself county respectability and enjoy the mystique attached to English landed estates by purchasing a county property. His vast and impersonal house in Grosvenor Square bespeaks his emptiness. Visiting the Melmottes in hope of catching a prosperous mate in their company, Georgiana Longestaffe reflects that her family's house in Bruton Street

> had never been very bright, but the appendages of life there had been of a sort which was not known in the gorgeous mansion in Grosvenor Square. It had been full of books and little toys and those thousand trifling household gods which are accumulated in years, and which in their accumulation suit themselves to the taste of their owners. In Grosvenor Square there were no Lares; – no toys, no books, nothing but gold and grandeur, pomatum, powder and pride. (I, 296)

The estate Melmotte proposes to buy in order to become a local squire is 'Pickering Park, the magnificent Sussex property of Adolphus Longestaffe, Esq., of Caversham' (I, 325), the money to be divided between Dolly Longestaffe and his father. The firm of Slow and Bideawhile is on the job as the

Longestaffe solicitors. Acting with their usual combination of intense probity and inefficiency, they allow themselves this time to arrange the sale without securing payment:

> The magnificence of Mr. Melmotte affected even the Longestaffe lawyers. Were I to buy a little property, some humble cottage with a garden, – or you, O reader, unless you be magnificent, – the money to the last farthing would be wanted, or security for the money more than sufficient, before we should be able to enter in upon our new home. But money was the very breath of Melmotte's nostrils, and therefore his breath was taken for money.   (I, 325)

However, the conflict of generations and ways of doing things, marked in the contrast between Roger Carbury and Melmotte, extends to Dolly and his father, and Dolly decides not to put up with Melmotte's evasiveness. His exasperated father asks, "'Why can't you trust Mr. Bideawhile? Slow and Bideawhile have been the family lawyers for a century." Dolly made some remark as to the old family advisers which was by no means pleasing to the father's ears, and went his way. The father knew his boy, and knew that his boy would go to Squercum' (II, 69).

Squercum is to solicitors what Chaffanbrass is to barristers, dirty and ill-turned-out, 'with putty-formed features, a squat nose, a large mouth, and very bright blue eyes . . . and many among his enemies said that he was a Jew' (II, 70–1). But he succeeds. Dolly likes him because he has 'no hesitation in supporting the interests of sons against those of their fathers. . . . There were some who, no doubt, would have liked to crush a man who was at once so clever, and so pestilential. But he had not as yet been crushed, and had become quite in vogue with elder sons' (II, 70). Though he is a sign of the times (bad times, Trollope would suggest), he is active and astute, 'making himself detestably odious among the very respectable clerks in Mr. Bideawhile's office, – men who considered themselves to be altogether superior to Squercum himself in professional standing' (II, 72). His energetic investigation convinces him that Dolly's signature to a letter surrendering the title deeds of the Pickering property has been forged by Melmotte. And that conviction eventually

brings Melmotte down. When, in the end, the proceeds from
the winding-up of Melmotte's affairs give Dolly a sizeable
bank account, he explains the new model of a *modus vivendi*
between a gentleman and his solicitor:

> 'I shall just make Squercum allow me so much a month,
> and I shall have all the bills and that kind of thing sent to
> him, and he will do everything, and pull me up if I'm getting
> wrong. I like Squercum.'
> 'Won't he rob you, old fellow?' suggested Nidderdale.
> 'Of course he will; – but he won't let anyone else do it. One
> has to be plucked, but it's everything to have it done on a
> system. If he'll only let me have ten shillings out of every
> sovereign I think I can get along.'   (II, 400–1)

As often happens in Trollope, a providential movement of
circumstances brings about a satisfactory conclusion despite
his complaint that lawyers are becoming sharp and shady and
that social values and the world in general are going to the
dogs. Mrs Hurtle, the wildcat American, joins forces with
Roger Carbury, and Mr Squercum, far more than the
Bidewhiles, prevents Melmotte's usurpation of the intangible dignities of a country estate. However, as Burke reminds
us that 'the state ought not to be considered as nothing better
than a partnership agreement in a trade of pepper and coffee,
calico or tobacco, or some other such low concern,'[16] Mr
Bidewhile informs Melmotte that estates transcend commerce: '"You must be aware, Mr. Melmotte," said the lawyer,
"that the sale of a property is not like an ordinary mercantile
transaction"' (II, 237). It is, nevertheless, Squercum whose
tenacity defeats Melmotte. And in the end, though in a different register, Dolly's expression of satisfaction with his solicitor
has a staunchness about it sufficiently reminiscent of Lord
Fawn's faith in Camperdown: '"If you knew," says Dolly, "the
comfort of having a fellow who could keep you straight without
preaching sermons at you you wouldn't despise Squercum. I've
tried to go alone and I find that does not answer. Squercum's
my coach, and I mean to stick pretty close to him"' (II, (431).
  Though Trollope's general historical sense that the solicitor's profession was going downhill may be wrong, and though
he may number among his attorneys some scoundrels like

Dockwrath, his account of the psychological bond of solicitor and client, and his depiction of the solicitor as guardian spirit defending more than the monetary concerns of the estate seem persuasive and close to what lawyers themselves have to say on the subject. As might be expected, he is shrewd in discerning moral and social discriminations within the profession, but most interesting, perhaps, is his evocation of the irrational, intangible Englishness of estates and the system of law that governs and protects them.

5   The Law and Politics

It is not surprising that students of the law, who in their occupation are necessarily closely interested in the rules laid down by society for the practical conduct of affairs in the world, should also desire to become lawmakers. Moreover, election to Parliament led to an enhanced career for lawyers either in the practice of their profession or in the distinguished appointments for which their backgrounds made them likely candidates. In *The New Zealander* Trollope notes with some disapproval the great number of lawyers in Parliament. As J. R. Vincent observes in his account of Victorian lawyers in Parliament: 'Every century has found to its chagrin that the House of Commons became a fifth Inn of Court'.[1] Concerning himself so keenly as a novelist in the delineation of political careers, Trollope naturally shows law as a stepping stone to political office and political office as a stepping stone to the higher reaches of the law. Occasionally the two spheres of interest combine intimately as in the lives of the Law Officers of the Crown, of whom Trollope creates several impressive examples, one of them, perhaps, his most intriguing and positive portait of a lawyer. He examines the link between law and politics in all its stages. Frank Greystock is a young lawyer making a career in politics; Phineas Finn one who attains high political office; Sir Gregory Grogram, Timothy Beeswax, Sir Abraham Haphazard, and Sir William Patterson are Attorneys and Solicitors-General. Moreover, the law as it affects election to office captures Trollope's attention as it did that of Victorians generally, electoral corruption being a topic of heated concern and constant reform throughout the century. He learned all about it at first hand when he stood for election at Beverley and later gave evidence at a trial to disallow the election. In all these matters, he is interested in the acquisition and exercise of power and status and in accomodations or tensions between private scruple and public office.

I shall look first at Trollope's epitome of the advocate-politician in his *Life of Cicero*, then at the connections he explores between law and politics in the nineteenth century (in the light of nineteenth-century legal history), then at his representation of some Law Officers of the Crown, and finally at his most intriguing full-scale depiction of one of them, the Solicitor-General, Sir William Patterson in *Lady Anna*.

In Trollope's *Life of Cicero* (1880), as Ruth ap Roberts observes, 'one may find the literal and discursive formulation of the attitudes that make the novels what they are'.[2] For Cicero, 'That career which led the great Romans up from the state of Quaestor, to the Aedile's, Praetor's, and Consul's chair, and thence to the rich reward of provincial govern-ment, was held to be the highest then open to the ambition of man' (I, 24). Similarly Trollope considers political life the pinnacle of aspiration, and election to Parliament 'an entrance into that assembly which by the consent of all men is the greatest in the world' (*PF*, I, 35). Admission to the Bar is a familiar first step towards that great assembly. For the paper barrister like Phineas Finn, who is admitted to the Bar but does not practice, the law may then have served its purpose. But if election to Parliament were insufficient in itself to satisfy ambition, a lawyer might hope to become a Law Officer of the Crown: a Solicitor or Attorney-General. If very distin-guished in the law and politics, he might hope (as Sir Gregory Grogram hopes in *The Prime Minister*) to be nominated by the Prime Minister to ascend the woolsack as Lord Chancellor and thus become the Keeper of the King's conscience, the leading subject in the land after the Royal Family and the Archbishop of Canterbury.

Just as in Trollope's world where 'the highest work of a lawyer can only be reached through political struggle' (*ED*, 34), advocacy was Cicero's entryway to political office, and he continued his vocation as an advocate throughout his political career. 'He wished, no doubt, to shine as does the barrister of to-day; he wished to rise; he wished if you will to make his fortune, – not by the taking of fees but by extending himself into higher influence by the authority of his name' (I, 29). His extraordinary power as an orator was the cornerstone of success in both arenas, in the senate as in the courts.

Having a sceptical view of lawyers in general, it is on Cicero's stature as orator that Trollope focuses in order to raise Cicero above the ruck of common lawyers. About Cicero's *Pro Murena*, he says: 'the best morsel in the whole oration is that in which he snubs the lawyers. It must be understood that Cicero did not pride himself on being a lawyer. He was an advocate, and if he wanted law there were those of an inferior grade to whom he could go to get it' (I, 232). Though Trollope compares Cicero with English barristers frequently throughout the book, nevertheless, 'we learn that a Roman advocate was by no means the same as an English barrister. The science which he was supposed to have learned was simply that of telling his story in effective language . . . he looked elsewhere, to men of another profession, for his law' (I, 233). All very well, but consider what Trollope has said of the English advocate's legal learning in *The Eustace Diamonds*:

> The best of the legal profession consists in this; – that when you get fairly at work you may give over working. An aspirant must learn everything; but a man may make his fortune at it, and know almost nothing. He may examine a witness with judgment, see through a case with precision, address a jury with eloquence, – and yet be altogether ignorant of law. . . . The men whose names are always in the newspapers never look at their Stone and Toddy, – care for it not at all, – have their Stone and Toddy got up for them by their juniors when cases require that reference shall be made to precedents. . . . Greystock never thought of the law now, unless he had some special case in hand. (205–6)

The point of difference between English barristers and Cicero looks rather like a point of resemblance. Still, Trollope is coming near to suggesting that Greystock is a conceited dilettante. And lest a similar thought about Cicero occur to the reader of the *Life*, he adds, 'But in truth few men understood the Roman law better than did Cicero' (I, 234).

The fusion of lawyer and politician in Cicero, however, is more than a matter of skill with words. In a significant way, law is the subject of the *Life of Cicero*, the disintegrating law of the Roman republic. Trollope's interest is in the idea of a man with good intentions, and a good many personal weaknesses, trying to bolster and maintain the laws of a republic that, once noted for severe probity, had now for various reasons of greed, status and cowardice abandoned law and would invoke it only as a convenient facade to disguise base motives:

> Cicero had conceived a Republic in his own mind, – not Utopian, altogether human and rational, – a Republic which he believed to have been that of Scipio, of Marcellus, and Laelius, a Republic which should do nothing for him but require his assistance, in which the people should vote and the oligarchs rule in accordance with the established laws.   (II, 274)

'His words', says Trollope, 'did more than armies, but neither could do anything lasting for the Republic' (II, 273). The republic he thought to maintain was not the decrepit republic that now existed.

> In this consists the charm of his character, though at the same time the weakness of his political aspirations; his weakness, – because he was vain enough to imagine that he could talk men back from their fishponds; its charm, – because he was able through it all to believe in honesty (II, 273)

In the political novels, Trollope lays bare all the moral and psychological nuances in place-seeking, the exercise of power, and direction of human affairs and explores the intricate relationship of private and public life, measuring personal and political conduct in accordance with his touchstones of honesty and truth. In Cicero he finds rich ground for all these concerns – the more so as Trollope's contemporaries had found Cicero wanting in honesty, modesty, candour and courage. In 1863 the distinguished barrister and man of letters, William Forsyth, author of *Hortensius*, a history of advocacy named after Cicero's great rival in the law, and a

History of Trial by Jury, wrote a *Life of Cicero*. He and Trollope clearly shared many interests – Forsyth had also written a book on the *Novels and Novelists of the Eighteenth Century* – but in his own *Life of Cicero*, Trollope repeatedly finds fault with Forsyth's estimate of Cicero's character and advocacy. Given Trollope's long-standing preoccupation with the ethics of advocacy, it is not surprising that he should devote considerable attention to Cicero's honesty as an advocate in the defence of bad causes. Despite his sympathy for Cicero, Trollope remains consistent in his attitude toward lawyers, condemning what he takes to be the advocate's duplicity, though, in this case, he makes such allowance as he can: Cicero had not 'progressed far enough in modern civilization to have studied the beauty of truth' (I, 126); 'he was as right at any rate as the modern barrister' (I, 30); and

> When I look at the practice of our times, I find that thieves and rebels are defended by honourable advocates, who do not scruple to take their briefs in opposition to their own opinions. It suited Cicero to do the same. If I were detected in a plot for blowing up a Cabinet Council I do not doubt that I should get the late Attorney-General to defend me (I, 256).

If Cicero's status as an orator raises him above mere lawyers, oratory too harbours within itself a traditional weakness. Cicero's performance, whether as advocate or political orator, is tainted in Trollope's eyes by a flaw fundamentally serious but understandable within the system of rhetoric that Cicero inherited:

> All Cicero's treatises on the subject [of eloquence] and Quintillian's, and those of the pseudo-Tacitus, and of the first Greek from which they have come, fall to the ground as soon as we are told that it must be the purport of the orator to turn the mind of those who hear him either to the right or to the left, in accordance with the drift of the cause. . . . It cannot be right to make another man believe that which you think to be false. (II, 317)

This is the core of the matter.

To make the men who heard him believe in him was the one gift which Cicero valued; – not to make them know him to be true, but to believe him to be so. . . . he had not acquired that theoretic aversion to a lie which is the first feeling in the bosom of a modern gentleman. (II, 335)

The point about Cicero's inherited rhetorical tradition of false persuasion is interesting as an enlargement of Trollope's familiar complaint against advocates but also as making a connection between advocacy and politics. Both are vitally concerned with persuasion in difficult circumstances. The twisting, turning, and manoeuvering which Trollope portrays so astutely in, for example, *The Prime Minister* is aimed at persuading reluctant people to co-operate towards a common aim. Persuasion becomes a mere instrument for holding on to power. Near the end of his term as Prime Minister even Plantagenet, 'this Aristides' (II, 326), loses his grip on the truth, holding on to power for its own sake and refusing to see that his government's work is done and that he must resign – 'The poison of place and power and dignity had got into his blood' (II, 315).

Ultimately, Cicero's misfortune was that with humanity, moderation and a general honesty befitting a Christian, he 'had not risen to that appreciation of the beauty of truth which an exercise of Christianity is supposed to exact' (II, 133). The *Life of Cicero* gave Trollope, perhaps, his fullest opportunity for investigating the relationship of lawyer and lawmaker and for exploring the psychological and moral quandaries of the lawyer as politician.

II

From Trollope's general views about the combination of law and politics, clearly and consistently presented in the *Life of Cicero*, let us turn to his particular depiction of lawyer politicians and those occasions when contemporary law directly affects the political process.

Two sorts of barristers make their way into Parliament as into business, the 'paper' barrister and the barrister in earnest. The paper barrister acquires a practical knowledge of affairs and a legal training such as may be useful to a commercial firm or in various other types of administration or teaching, and though he is called to the Bar does not practise as a lawyer. The convenience of this state of affairs was recognised early in the Inns of Court and of Chancery. Some of the most distinguished families sent their children there, not necessarily to become lawyers, but to prepare for practical life in a social and professional career. Sir John Fortescue (c.1394–c.1476), Lord Chief Justice of the King's Bench and 'gubernator' of Lincoln's Inn in 1425, 1426 and 1429, shows how the studies stretched to accommodate such prospects: 'There is,' he says,

> both in the inns of court, and the inns of chancery, a sort of academy, or gymnasium, fit for the persons of their station; where they learn signing, and all kinds of music, dancing and such other accomplishments and diversions (which are called revels) as are suitable to their quality, and such as are usually practiced at court.[3]

In the history of English literature, perhaps the most eminent graduate of this training was Geoffrey Chaucer. In *Some New Light on Chaucer*, John Manly notes that Chaucer was educated at the Inner Temple (one of the Inns of Court) in 'those legal studies which furnished the best training then accessible for a career as government official or man of business', and suggests that his various court appointments (Controller of Customs, diplomat on missions concerned with commercial treaties, Clerk of the King's Works at Westminster Palace and elsewhere, Sub-Forester of the King's Park in North Petherton) were not plums handed out in recognition of his poetry but appointments suitable to his practical training and accomplishment.[4] The same situation prevailed in the nineteenth century. As Duman points out in his excellent study of *The English and Colonial Bars in the Nineteenth Century*, the Inns played a very significant role in preparing young men for positions in the governing elite of the country: 'Here ambitious men gained entrance to a high-status professional fraternity, became masters of specialized legal knowledge and of skills that would be invaluable assets in the House of Commons, were inculcated with the norms of the governing classes and made potentially useful social and political connections.'⁵ Election to the House was a great asset for an ambitious barrister either in politics or the law. Duman shows that of fifty-four barristers elected to the House in 1880, two-thirds achieved at least one professional appointment. And he concludes: 'In the light of this overwhelming evidence there can be little doubt that 'legal careerists' were entirely correct in viewing the House of Commons as the high road to office, to profit and to power.'⁶ Barristers were the largest professional group in the House. Between 1815 and 1914, 21 per cent of cabinet ministers had been called to the Bar, and many of the foremost political figures, such as Peel, Disraeli and Gladstone, had been students at an Inn.⁷ In Trollope's time most of the barrister politicians were Liberals, and only slightly more than 10 per cent of the barrister ministers were sons or grandsons of peers or baronets – most were from the urban middle classes. Thus, says Duman, they 'were the cuckoos in the nineteenth-century political nest'.⁸

Trollope's Phineas Finn fits this general pattern. Chaucer was a vintner's son, Phineas is an Irish country doctor's. The doctor pays 'the usual fee to a very competent and learned gentleman in the Middle Temple' and allows his son 'one hundred and fifty pounds per annum for three years'. Phineas shows no special aptitude: 'no evidence came home as to the acquirement of any considerable amount of law lore, or even as to much law study' (*PF*, I, 3). From the start, though not by Mr Low, the Chancery barrister with whom he has been studying, Phineas is encouraged to see the law merely as an entrée:

> He had dined three or four times with that great Whig nobleman, the Earl of Brentford. And he had been assured that if he stuck to the English Bar he would certainly do well. Though he might fail to succeed in court or in chambers, he would doubtless have given to him some one of those numerous appointments for which none but clever young barristers are supposed to be fitting candidates. (I, 4)

When a friend suggests, after Phineas has been called to the Bar, that he stand for the Irish borough of Loughshane in an immediate election, the thought is tempting: 'He was already

a barrister, and there were so many things open to a barrister
with a seat in Parliament!' (I, 10).

His father takes a dimmer view – '"Stupid young fool! . . . I
wonder whether he has ever dreamed what he is to live upon"'
(I, 11). And Mr Low tells him upon his election that he has 'as
good as ruined himself' (I, 41). Low believes in barristers
becoming MP's, but only after succeeding in their profession:
'As a rule one never hears of a barrister going into Parliament
till after he's forty' (I, 52). Low's views are at least frightening,
but the law alone lacks glamour: 'A set of very dingy chambers
up two pairs of stairs at No. 9, Old Square, Lincoln's Inn, to
which Mr. Low had recommended him to transfer himself
and all his belongings, were waiting his occupation, should he
resolve upon occupying them' (I, 74). Choosing between law
and Parliament, Phineas gambles on Parliament, with a sop of
good intentions to ease his conscience: 'There were certain
books, – law books, – which he would read at such intervals of
leisure as politics might give him' (I, 79). It is hardly doubtful
that Phineas's charm for influential women such as Lady
Laura Standish stands him in much better stead than his
knowledge of the law.

Getting into Parliament involves election, and election, as
Trollope knew from experience, could well involve candidates in litigation. Corruption in elections had been a notorious subject of inquiry and legislation throughout the century.
As parliamentary reports and statutes show, electors were
virtually as spirited and ingenious in confounding Parliament's efforts at 'purity' as legislators were in trying to
impose it. 'The whole of the inhabitants of this borough,'
wrote William Cobbett about Honiton in 1806, 'the whole of
the persons who return two members to Parliament, are
bound together in an indissoluble chain of venality.' When he
protested to them about the evil of taking bribes, he says, 'they
cried out against me . . . as a man that had come to rob them of
their *blessing*.'[9] Placards at Bristol in 1832 exhorted 'Vote for
Blue. Money no object.'[10] Asa Briggs notes that 850 of the
1000 voters at Stafford in 1832 were bought, and things did
not change much after Reform: 'the 1841 Parliament was
known as the "Bribery Parliament", and more than ten years
later in 1852 the barrister-novelist, Samuel Warren, argued
that "bribery is seen perhaps in fuller action at the moment

than ever before, as is testified on all hands by those competent to form an opinion on the subject."' Tradition was strong. 'It is difficult', says Briggs, 'to determine to what extent corruption was the instrument candidates chose to "influence" the electorate and to what extent it sprang from the "wickedness" of the electors themselves.'[11] Virtue did not seem to shine more conspicuously from one group or class than another. Speaking of his practice in election petitions in the late sixties, the time of Trollope's experience as a candidate at Beverley, Serjeant Ballantine concludes: bribery was 'confined to no class – tradesmen, the squirearchy, the lawyers, and, by no means insignificantly, the clergy, all were implicated; and I cannot forbear to add that the amount of perjury necessary to conceal it was by no means deficient.'[12]

'Influence' took a variety of forms, landlord over tenant, employer over worker, customers over tradesmen. Drink and food were commonplace 'blessings.' Cash, as Trollope notes in *Ralph the Heir*, was paid out with a nice sense of market conditions: 'They always hang back,' growls the candidate Griffenbottom when at noon the going rate is three half-crowns, 'Fight it out.' Fighting it out has the consequence that by four o'clock 'the men have been getting as much as fifteen shillings a head!' (II, 13–14). Further irregularities included impersonation, bullying and abduction. In the general conduct and orchestration of the election, an election agent was the principal strategist.

If a petition were presented against the results of an election so influenced, a parliamentary committee heard the evidence and reported to the Speaker. If the corruption were profound, as at Sudbury in 1841, the recommendation might be not just for unseating but for a commission to consider disfranchising the borough. Awareness of that danger led to further kinds of collusion between the contending parties. Indeed, the procession of Acts and Reports of the 1840s and 1850s[13] 'for better discovery of bribery and corruption', and 'for more effectual inquiry into corrupt practices', suggests the degree of inventive wiliness in the corrupt that required these ever more efficient measures. The Corrupt Practices Act of 1854[14] was the first to define bribery and undue influence, assign penalties, and establish election auditors, though the act had limited effect. A considerable change in procedure occurred with the Parliamentary Elections Act of 1868[15] (the year Trollope stood for election at Beverley), which legislated the appointment of Common Law judges instead of parliamentary committees to try election petitions. 'The ground for this change', says Serjeant Ballantine, 'was the supposition that the inquiries before committees resulted too often in decisions founded less upon the facts than the composition of the tribunal; and this certainly had been the case in former years.'[16] Even with this change, a becoming gravity about such long-standing and widespread cheating was difficult to ensure. Trollope was right in *The Kellys and the O'Kellys* about 'the great difficulty of coming to a legal decision on a political question, in a criminal court' (16).

In the Beverley chapter of *An Autobiography*, Trollope discusses his disillusioning experience as a candidate for election in November 1868. A petition followed the Beverley election and Trollope gave testimony. It seems likely from the language and incidents of Trollope's fictional elections that he had not only his own experience to go on but an acquaintance with the statutes and reports I have mentioned.[17] Moreover, the whole experience of electoral corruption, petition and trial was undergone the same year at Taunton by Trollope's friend and fellow member of the Garrick Club, the eminent barrister, Sir Henry James. During his campaign, Sir Henry made declarations about bribery to the voters similar to those made by Trollope's Mr Underwood,[18] and, like Phineas at Tankerville, gained the seat by petition after losing the election. He subsequently became Solicitor and Attorney-General and in 1883 drafted and carried the Corrupt Practices bill. At the petition trial, he was represented by Serjeant Ballantine and unseated Serjeant Cox. Charles Merewether, the barrister who aided Trollope by writing the opinion on heirlooms for *The Eustace Diamonds*, also stood for election, as a Conservative, in 1868 at Northampton and lost. He was elected in 1874, 'a thoroughly true blue Church and State Tory, of the no progress kind',[19] and later, in 1880, became a commissioner to inquire into corrupt practices at elections.

Whatever personal feelings the Beverley contest prompted in him, for one so interested in the English way of doing things, and nostalgic, as his treatment of estates shows, for feudal relationships, Trollope had an excellent subject in misbehaviour at elections. Although Phineas, contemplating the lightness with which such chicanery and illegality are regarded, concludes: 'There is no honesty in the life we lead' (*PR*, II, 45), Trollope avoids reducing what may seem to us a clear-cut moral issue to a matter of black and white. At Beverley, as he tells in *An Autobiography*, he was surprised by his agent's greeting:

> Oh no! . . . you won't get in. I don't suppose you really expect it. But there is a fine career open to you. You will spend £1000, and lose the election. Then you will petition, and spend another £1000. You will throw out the elected members. There will be a commission, and the borough will be disfranchised. For a beginner such as you are, that will be a great success.   (298–300)

Mr Underwood in *Ralph the Heir* (I, 235) and Phineas in *Phineas Redux* (I, 15–16) are treated to virtually the same words. Trollope's surprise at this neat summary of political manoeuvring suggests an initial degree of *naïveté*, for, in fact, as G. M. Young and W. D. Handcock point out, 'Election petitions were not necessarily the fruits of outraged purity; more often they were part of the regular tactics of the game, or arose out of spite and vindictiveness.'[20] Griffenbottom in *Ralph the Heir* is an old hand: 'He had petitioned and been petitioned against' (I, 237). And the novel presents the whole route from petition and unseating to a commission of inquiry to disfranchisement, a process doing neither party any good except that two Conservative seats are wiped out. In *Phineas Redux* the tactical manoeuvre is somewhat clearer and works, even though Ruddles, Phineas's agent, has had a qualm or two about refraining from a little counter-bribery. Seeing the price of Conservative votes rising, Ruddles exults: 'We shall carry the seat on a scrutiny as sure as eggs' (I, 44).

The object in such manoeuvring was to unseat the opposition and gain the seat for one's own party, as Phineas does when his opponent's corrupt votes are subtracted from the poll as a result of a petition trial. The judge recommends a commission to look into Tankerville's corruption at elections, present and past, and the commission recommends prosecution of Phineas's opponent, Browborough. It stops short of recommending disfranchisement of the borough, however, so Phineas keeps the seat. An example of less successful strategy was the famous corrupt election at Sudbury in 1841. The report of the commissioners resulted in a bill for disfranchisement which passed in the Commons but failed in the Lords because the townsmen, who had been content enough to give evidence invalidating the election, refused to repeat their evidence for the Lords when the issue became complete disfranchisement. A new committee was set up only to encounter a remarkable and general amnesia among the townsmen: 'Not only was no disposition manifested on their part to assist in carrying out the object and intent of the Legislature in appointing such a Commission, but there appeared on all sides a settled purpose to defeat that object.'[21] Immunity had been offered to witnesses, but the Legislature had unfortunately also stated that no one should be compelled to give evidence – so the townsmen chose silence. One tradesman, 'for the benefit . . . of the freemen', exhibited the Legislative provisos for non-compulsion in his shop-window.[22] 'All party feeling', wrote the indignant commissioners, 'was merged in one common desire to preserve the franchise, which was supposed to be endangered by the investigation.'[23] Such staunch communal spirit did no good. The borough was disfranchised.

One feature of the Sudbury election as described by the commissioners, and no doubt often repeated – the matter of the disappearing henchman – shows up in Trollope's Percy-cross. At Sudbury, three strangers had dispensed bribes, but 'These strangers left a few hours after the election, and have never been seen there since. . . . Their names and residence are equally unknown to the inhabitants; and after the most diligent inquiry we could obtain no clue to any of them.'[24] In *Ralph the Heir*, their counterpart is the mysterious Glump:

Trigger [Mr Underwood's agent] was ready to swear that he did not know whence Glump had got the money, and Glump himself was, – nobody knew where Glump was, but strange whispers respecting Glump were floating about the borough. Trigger was disposed to believe that they, on their side, could prove that Glump had really been employed by Westmacott's people to vitiate the election. He was quite

sure that nothing could connect Glump with him as an
agent on behalf of Griffenbottom and Underwood. . . . It
was the general impression through the borough that
Glump had on this occasion been hired by Trigger, and
Trigger certainly enjoyed the prestige which was thus conferred upon him.   (II, 183)

Dropping a petition could be as much a matter of strategy as
initiating it. Both the Report of the Select Committee of 1842
on Election Proceedings and the Act for Better Discovery of
Bribery and Corruption (1842) address themselves to collusion and compromise between winners and losers for the
withdrawal of petitions. In a situation, such as that in *Ralph the
Heir*, where a petition was launched against two successful
candidates of the same party, an agreement might be reached
whereby, in return for dropping the petition, one of the
victors would vacate his seat and be replaced by an unopposed
member of the opposite party at the election resulting from
the vacancy. Thus, both a likely disfranchisement and considerable expense in litigation might be avoided. The 1842
Select Committee Report documents such an agreement with
all its elaborate provisos and conditions. Percycross is quite
used to such arrangements. Aware of the increasing weight of
legislation against corrupt practices, indeed marvelling 'that
the borough should have escaped so long', the 'wise men at
Percycross had concluded that it would be better, just for the
present, to let things run smoothly, and to return their two old
members' (that is, one Conservative and one Liberal). 'Foolish'
heads prevail, however, and the seats are contested (I, 234–5).
When Underwood and Griffenbottom face a petition, various
accommodations are suggested. 'Mr. Spicer certainly had
friends who might be conducive to the withdrawal of petition,'
if Underwood would take some political action to the advantage of Mr Spicer's mustard business (II, 121). Again, 'If Sir
Thomas Underwood would prevail on Lord —— to appoint
Mr. O'Blather to the vacant office [of postmaster], then all the
Givantake influence at Percycross should be used towards the
withdrawal of the petition' (II, 124). Then Mr Trigger puts the
classic compromise to Underwood: 'If we go on it will lead to
disfranchising the borough. . . . The Liberals only want one
seat. If you'll undertake to accept the Hundreds, the petition

will be withdrawn, and Mr. Westmacott will come forward again. In that case we shouldn't oppose' (II, 130–1).[25] But Sir Thomas, determinedly upright, will not consent to make all comfortable. And Mr Griffenbottom concludes in great disgust: 'This comes of bringing a gentleman learned in the law down into the borough' (II, 135).

With his characteristic all-round vision, Trollope not only presents the moral viewpoint legislators attempted to impose but also the traditionally inherited arguments for bribery that made it so hard to extinguish. Sir Thomas champions 'purity' as Trollope had at Beverley. 'There was something grand', says Trollope in *An Autobiography*, 'in the scorn with which a leading Liberal there turned up his nose at me when I told him that there should be no bribery, no treating, not even a pot of beer on our side!' (306). Sir Thomas gets like respect: 'Sir Thomas had made himself very odious even to Mr. Griffenbottom himself' (II, 3). Mr Pile, the local bootmaker, however, expresses a more traditional attitude, and raises the question why one should vote for an outsider. Trollope himself seems to have been untroubled by the representational role of a member of Parliament and more irritated at having to put up with the ways of strangers who should elect him than curious about why they should elect a stranger. Mr Pile touches that point: 'that a stranger should come to the borough and want the seat without paying for it was to him so distasteful that this assurance [of purity] from the mouth of one of the candidates did make him very sick' (I, 244). He elaborates:

And what's the meaning of it all? It's just this, – that folks wants what they wants without paying for it. I hate Purity, I do. I hate the very smell of it. It stinks. When I see the chaps as come here and talk of Purity, I know they mean that nothing ain't to be as it used to be. Nobody is to trust no one. There ain't to be nothing warm, nor friendly, nor comfortable any more. (I, 314–15)

This is cash-nexus in an unexpected light. Pile, in his way, is arguing for community, feudal bonds, and loyalty. As Young and Handcock say, 'If electors were generally prepared to

regard themselves as politically infeudated to their social and
economic betters, reciprocal services were expected.'[26] So Pile

> loved bribery in his very heart. But it is equally true that he
> did not want to be bribed himself. It was the old-fashioned
> privilege of a poor man to receive some small consideration
> for his vote in Percycross, and Mr. Pile could not endure to
> think that the poor man should be robbed of his little
> comforts.   (II, 4)

Moreover, Trollope gives Pile a special sanction. Vehemently
opposed as Pile and Underwood are on the issue of bribery,
'There was a species of honesty about Mr. Pile which almost
endeared him to Sir Thomas' (II, 129). And the feeling of
decency is reciprocated when Underwood, rejecting schemes
of compromise and collusion put forward by a group from
Percycross, dismisses the deputation:

> 'Unfriendly,' said Mr Griffenbottom with a sneer.
> 'Goodbye, Sir Thomas,' said Mr. Pile, putting out his
> hand. Sir Thomas shook hands with Mr. Pile cordially. 'It's
> my opinion that he's right,' said Mr. Pile. 'I don't like his
> notions but I do like his pluck. Good-bye, Sir Thomas.'
> (II, 136)

Such feudal nostalgia as clings to Mr Pile's notions of bribery
is, in Mr Browborough of *Phineas Redux*, stripped down to a
single tenuous idea of gentlemanly conduct: that he pays up.
'How should a Browborough get a seat without buying it, – a
man who could not say ten words, of no family, with no
natural following in any constituency, distinguished by no zeal
in politics, entertaining no special convictions of his own? . . .
he had gone to Tankerville with money in his hand, with
plenty of money, and had spent it – like a gentleman.' The
phrase, 'like a gentleman', reflects the wishful thoughts of
many parliamentarians who, having gained their own seats by
bribery, can summon up only a *pro forma* sort of indignation
on the subject. 'Collectively the House of Commons had
determined to put down bribery with a very strong hand.
Nobody had spoken against bribery with more fervour than
Sir Gregory Grogram, who had himself, as Attorney-General,

forged the chains for fettering future bribers.' But Sir Gregory's own election was lubricated by plenty of beer, and though he prosecutes Browborough, 'it was observed by many that the job was not much to his taste.' The burning indignation of the House, says Trollope, coincides with 'a slight undercurrent of ridicule attaching itself to the question of which only they who were behind the scenes were conscious' (II, 33).

Browborough's trial is therefore a tongue-in-cheek affair – 'his safety lay in the indifference of his prosecutors' (II, 36). Not just indifference, but a good deal of indulgent irony prevails. 'A considerable amount of gentle fun was poked at the witnesses by the defending counsel,' and 'a large amount of good-humoured sparring was allowed' (II, 39). The advocates drop their customary tone of wrathful righteousness. 'The general flavour of the trial at Durham was one of good-humoured raillery.' As for Sir Gregory's prosecution, there is 'nothing more eloquent than his denunciations against bribery in general; nothing more mild than his allegations against Mr. Browborough individually' (II, 38). The verdict is for acquittal, a surprise to no-one 'unless it might be some poor innocents here and there about the country who had been induced to believe that bribery and corruption were in truth to be banished from the purlieus of Westminister' (II, 40).

It might be thought that Trollope's viewpoint is soured here by events at Beverley, and that he is exaggerating for the sake of art. Halperin concedes, 'Of course this is a fairy-tale trial.'[27] But Serjeant Ballantine, whose experience of trials resulting from corrupt elections was extensive, gives an account precisely similar to Trollope's. Ballantine was, in fact, counsel for the respondents at Beverley and thus, perhaps, the model for Trollope's Serjeant Burnaby. He also acted for Trollope's friend, Sir Henry James, in a petition trial of the same year that unseated his opponent and gave Sir Henry the seat. Ballantine's account is worth quoting at length:

> The tribunals were extremely pleasant to practice before, and the members that constituted them certainly were very competent to judge of the facts, having had their own experiences to be guided by, and within my observation an excellent feeling prevailed between them and counsel. I do

not think that there existed so holy a horror for bribery as
ought to affect well-regulated minds; in fact, the war waged
against Parliamentary corruption does not seem to have
attained either practical or moral success [Ballantine's book
was published in 1882], and an ordinarily acute observer
must come to the consclusion that the virtuous denunciations he hears are in most instances shams. There is no force
of public opinion honestly brought to bear against it. I
should be glad to know whether the gentry in the neighbourhood have ever withdrawn their custom from a tradesman found guilty of accepting bribes, or whether any gentleman has been excluded from society because he has given
them. Only during the present year I had the honour of
being associated with the Attorney-General in the prosecution of some bribery informations tried at Maidstone. A
solicitor, a leading one in the county, was called as a witness.
He had been obliged to make a clean breast of it before the
commissioners. He mounted the witness-box with a jaunty
air, and, with a complacent smile upon his countenance,
disclosed the organised system of bribery of which he had
been contriver and manager. I doubt whether a single client
will take his title-deeds out of this gentleman's possession,
or treat him with less consideration. Another witness got
up, he was one of the bribed, and was attended by several of
his friends and co-bribees – I invent the word for the
occasion. He gave his evidence in a jocular manner, and it
was listened to with much hilarity and evident admiration.
Even in the House of Commons, where a good deal of
verbal indignation is ventilated, the true feeling crept out
upon a recent occasion, when the majority refused to issue a
commission in a case where, according to public rumour,
bribery and corruption had been rampant.[28]

Is that not Trollope's world to the life?

　　Trollope's personal experience at Beverley with its petition
trial and commission of inquiry gave him extensive knowledge of electoral corruption, including scenes perhaps too
remarkable for fiction, as when Trollope's Conservative
opponent, Edwards, and Edwards's counsel interrupted the
Commission's proceedings at the town hall, declaring, as the
Commissioners reported, 'that they had as much right to
occupy the Town Hall as we, the Commissioners, had.' The

police superintendent seconded to the Commission sided with
the locals and refused to remove the obstructive parties,
whereupon 'a scene of uproar and disorder ensued', causing
the Commission to move to the Session House instead.[29] The
Commissioners reported that

> out of a constituency of something over 1,100, at the date of
> the Representation of the People Act, 1867, about 800 were
> open to bribery and other corrupt influences, there being in
> the constituency a body of about 300 without political
> principles or political likings or dislikings of any kind,
> locally known as 'rolling stock,' and about 250 others on
> either side, who, if money were going, expected to be paid,
> and would not vote unless they were paid or received some
> assurance that they would be paid after the election.[30]

The voters looked upon money as a bribe only if it came from
a candidate or party other than their own. In all, about a
thousand voters received payment.

Trollope clearly had a fine spectacle to study. His language,
however, also shows a familiarity with the terminology of the
bribery statutes, especially the Act of 1854: 'personation of
votes', 'undue influence', 'treating', 'intimidation' – common
enough terms but headings which he ticks off one after
another in the petition trial of *Ralph the Heir* (II, 182–5) and
which were not so mentioned at Beverley. We may, therefore,
reasonably assume, I think, that he read and added such legal
lore to his own experience – it would be natural after all that,
faced with the inquiry at Beverley, he would inform himself of
the law.

It has often been noted that Trollope's views of law, government, commerce and social mores in general became more
sombre as he grew older. Occasionally, as in the behaviour of
Old Bailey barristers, the historical trend was actually opposite
to what he perceived. On the subject of bribery, however, his
views seem generally sound, though ironically, with the coming
of the secret ballot (which he opposed) and the increasing
power and organisation of political parties, electoral corruption was soon to diminish most markedly. We can, however, see
once again how Trollope uses legal processes to articulate the
moral workings in society. We see society in the formulation,
exercise and contemplation of law, making up its collective

mind with considerable doubt and misgiving. The very legislators so publicly vehement for the law they have made are far
from enthusiastic about its particular enforcement. Trollope's
accomplishment here seems to me very considerable.

III

Having been elected, a barrister might look forward to one of
the desirable political appointments for which his skills made
him a likely candidate, or he might, since the House met in the
evening, continue both as a practising lawyer and a member of
Parliament, or he might become a Law Officer of the Crown.
The categories were not exclusive. Plantagenet Palliser tells his
son in *The Duke's Children*:

> 'If I were to name the class of men whose lives are spent with
> the most thorough enjoyment, I think I should name that of
> barristers who are in large practice and also in Parliament.'
>   'Isn't it a great grind, sir?' asked Silverbridge.
>   'A very great grind, as you call it. And there may be the
> grind and not the success. . . . But it is the grind that makes
> the happiness. To feel that your hours are filled to over-
> flowing, that you can barely steal minutes enough for sleep,
> that the welfare of many is entrusted to you, that the world
> looks on and approves, that some good is always being done
> to others, – above all things some good to your country; –
> that is happiness.' (I, 238–9)

The Attorney-General and the Solicitor-General, the Law
Officers of the Crown, perhaps best exemplify the Duke's
idealistic outlook here. They represent and advise the sovereign and the government, give opinions on international and
constitutional law, and advise departments of government.
The Attorney-General has been titular head of the English
Bar since 1814, the Solicitor-General his assitant and deputy.
As a reward for political service, they have a traditional right
of judicial preferment and may look forward to becoming
Lord Chancellor, Lord Chief Justice or Master of the Rolls,
though such expectations are not always fulfilled. The modern reader may detect what seems an oddity, reflected in the
Duke's remarks above, in the practice of Trollope's Law

Officers: unlike their modern counterparts, they have private practices in addition to their parliamentary responsibilities. The Attorney-General advises Mr Harding in *The Warden*, and Sir William Patterson, the Solicitor-General, acts in a lengthy inheritance case in *Lady Anna*. As J. Edwards observes in *The Law Officers of the Crown*, dissatisfaction about the indeterminate position of the Law Officers between private practice and state service appeared in the House of Commons about 1830.[31] Though called on by government offices to deal with legal questions, they had, in order to execute this governmental business, to use the staffs and resources they possessed as private practitioners. 'It was not until 1893 that a Law Officer's Department was established with a small secretarial staff.'[32] One notes that Trollope's Law Officers are well-off – they had to be. Moreover, their conduct of private cases might well have effects on their political careers, as we shall see in *Lady Anna*. Not until 1895 were they denied private practice.

One of Trollope's notable Law Officers is Sir Abraham Haphazard in *The Warden*. The Reverend Septimus Harding, a gentle clergyman, holds a sinecure as Warden of Hiram's Hospital, a foundation instituted in the fifteenth century to provide a home for twelve old men. The income greatly appreciates over the centuries, and John Bold, Harding's prospective son-in-law, creates a public outcry over what he takes to be mismanagement and exploitation on the part of the Church. Mr Harding, famous among Trollope's characters for the charitable delicacy of his conscience, is deeply concerned about his old men but agonised at the thought of being 'gorged with the wealth which the charity of former times has left for the solace of the aged' (10). He seeks, or receives, advice from three principal sources: his aged Bishop, the Bishop's son (and Harding's son-in-law), Archdeacon Grantly, and Sir Abraham Haphazard, Queen's Counsel and Attorney-General. :

It is interesting that Thomas L. Shaffer, Professor of Law at the University of Notre Dame, finds in *The Warden* a useful text for lawyers about the process of helping a client to make up his mind: 'My object', he says, ' . . . is to present Septimus Harding and his creator as teachers of lawyers.'[33] Shaffer's is a discussion valuable for its legal insight and for its focusing from a legal point of view on what is, after all, a major process

in all Trollope's novels, the intricate process of weighing the
pressures and nuances of various viewpoints in coming to a
decision. The passages he chooses to examine reveal, by the
way, a rhythmical system of similarities and contrasts that
contribute to the design of the book.

Mr Harding's concern is one which recurs many times in
Trollope's accounts of litigation: 'He was not so anxious to
prove himself right, as to be so' (35). His distinction, of course,
is between conscience, or justice, and legality. Archdeacon
Grantly, looks like

> a fitting impersonation of the church militant here on
> earth; . . . the broad chest, amply covered with fine cloth,
> told how well to do was its estate; one hand ensconced
> within his pocket, evinced the practical hold which our
> mother church keeps on her temporal possessions; and the
> other, loose for action, was ready to fight if need be in her
> defence . . .   (60–1).

When Mr Harding consults him, he is utterly exasperated at
any thought of yielding to a conscientious scruple. He hectors
and badgers his father-in-law as though Mr Harding were
barely responsible, treating him as a kind of moral simpleton,
especially when the warden's conscience moves him to resign.
'Such absurdity is enough to provoke Job,' Grantly tells his
wife while Harding stands meekly by. 'Your father is like a
child. Eight hundred pounds a year! – eight hundred and
eighty with the house – with nothing to do. The very place for
him. And to throw that up because some scoundrel writes an
article in a newspaper' (228). The Archdeacon, all bounce and
bluster, can barely listen to his father-in-law so bizarre does he
find the old man's qualms.

The consultation with Sir Abraham Haphazard ('What will
Sir Abraham think of it?' cries the Archdeacon. 'Did you not
know that it is not customary for clients to go direct to their
counsel? [223]), comes, interestingly, after Sir Abraham has
given his opinion in the case, and after Mr Harding has
virtually resolved to resign the wardenship. Trollope's description of Sir Abraham establishes a type that matches the
Duke's ideal of a parliamentary figure in all but spirit, and a
type worth keeping in mind for comparison with the later
portrait of Sir William Patterson.

He might be fifty years old, and would have looked young
for his age, had not constant work hardened his features,
and given him the appearance of a machine with a mind.
His face was full of intellect, but devoid of natural expression. You would say he was a man to use, and then have done
with; a man to be sought for on great emergencies, but ill
adapted for ordinary services; a man whom you would ask
to defend your property, but to whom you would be sorry to
confide your love. He was bright as a diamond, and as
cutting, and also as unimpressionable. He knew everyone
whom to know was an honour, but he was without a friend;
he wanted none, however, and knew not the meaning of the
word in other than its parliamentary sense. . . .
    With him success alone was praiseworthy, and he knew
none so successful as himself. No one had thrust him
forward; no powerful friends had pushed him along on his
road to power. No; he was attorney-general, and would, in
all human probability, be lord chancellor by sheer dint of
his own industry and his own talent. . . . And so he glitters
along through the world, the brightest among the bright;
and when his glitter is gone, and he is gathered to his
fathers, no eye will be dim with a tear, no heart will mourn
for its lost friend.   (213–15)

When Mr Harding asks if he is 'legally and distinctly entitled
to the proceeds of the property' (216), Haphazard evades the
question with a flurry of qualifications, but is brought up short
by Mr Harding's declaration that he can resign the wardenship.

    'What! throw it up altogether?' said the attorney-general,
gazing with utter astonishment at his client.
    . . . This poor little clergyman, cowed into such an act of
extreme weakness by a newspaper article, was to Sir
Abraham so contemptible an object, that he hardly knew
how to talk to him as to a rational being.   (217)

The interview ends with Mr Harding vehemently fingering
his imaginary cello as he asserts his conscience more clearly.
One is reminded of Uncle Toby and Sterne's reflections on
body-language. 'He was *standing up, gallantly fronting* Sir
Abraham, and his right arm passed with *bold and rapid* sweeps

before him, as though he were embracing some huge instrument, which allowed him *to stand thus erect*' (220,[my italics]). Leaving Sir Abraham's office, 'He stood still a moment to collect his thoughts. . . . He knew that the attorney-general regarded him as little better than a fool, but he did not mind' (221).

Drawing attention to the nicely matched counselling scenes in the novel, Professor Shaffer applies to them the psychiatrist Berne's patterns of conversational interaction. Both Archdeacon Grantly and Sir Abraham fail as counsellors by adopting a parent-to-child attitude of contemptuous superiority to Mr Harding. Their own notions of success prevent them from hearing his scruples with any understanding or sympathy. 'Counselling designed to help the client who is not interested so much in proving himself right as in being right,' says Shaffer, 'is difficult for one who is trained to be an advocate, and ally, and defender – trained, in other words, to be what the Archdeacon was to Septimus Harding, and, therefore, unable to provide comfort for his client's doubts.[34] Both advisers are bullies – because Sir Abraham's goals are personal and selfish, he is unable to extend to his client the freedom necessary for genuine choice in the client's moral and legal dilemma.[35]

In touching contrast, Mr Harding's old friend, the Bishop, though he points out principles and traditions that would allow Mr Harding to retain his post as warden, listens with respect and silent sympathy:

> The two old men were sitting near each other – so near that the Bishop was able to lay his hand upon the other's knee, and he did so with a gentle pressure. Mr. Harding knew well what that pressure meant. The Bishop had no further argument to adduce; he could not fight for the cause as his son would do; he could not prove all the precentor's doubts to be groundless; but he could sympathize with his friend, and he did so; and Mr. Harding felt that he had received that for which he came.   (38)

As Shaffer says, 'the most eloquent thing the Bishop did was *not* to talk. . . . Sometimes the best rule for a counselor is: Don't just do something; stand there.'[36]

The whole handling of the legal theme is characteristically Trollopian. Mr Harding's decision is made after the Attorney-General has, in one sense, effectively dealt with the case, not in substance but on a point of procedure. Sir Abraham finds that since, under the will, Mr Harding and Mr Chadwick (the steward) are 'only paid servants', they are not technically the correct defendants, and that as long as the plaintiffs fail to notice and alter this technical defect in the proceedings, the case will be lost. Grantly is delighted. '"That's excellent, Chadwick – that's excellent! I told you Sir Abraham was the man for us;" and he put down on the table the copy of the opinion, and patted it fondly' (101). He bestows on this lovely opinion the high honour of locking it away in that same private drawer in which he keeps his furtively treasured copy of Rabelais. Like Sir Abraham, Grantly appreciates the legal success – justice is the last thing on his mind.

> The archdeacon had again recourse to his drawer, and twice read through the essence of Sir Abraham Haphazard's law-enlightened and law-bewildered brains. It was very clear that to Sir Abraham, the justice of the old men's claim or the justice of Mr. Harding's defence were ideas that had never presented themselves. A legal victory over an opposing party was the service for which Sir Abraham was, as he imagined, to be paid; and that he, according to his lights, had diligently laboured to achieve, and with probable hope of success. Of the intense desire which Mr. Harding felt to be assured on fit authority that he was wronging no man, that he was entitled in true equity to his income, that he might sleep at night without pangs of conscience, that he was no robber, no spoiler of the poor; that he and all the world might be openly convinced that he was not the man which the *Jupiter* had described him to be; of such longings on the part of Mr. Harding, Sir Abraham was entirely ignorant. . . . Success was his object, and he was generally successful.
>
> The archdeacon was delighted with the closeness of the reasoning. To do him justice, it was not a selfish triumph that he desired; . . . but neither was it love of justice which made him so anxious, nor even mainly solicitude for his father-in-law. He was fighting a part of a never-ending

battle against a never-conquered foe – that of the church against its enemies.   (102–3)

In Sir Abraham, Trollope shows us a highly successful lawyer-politician, brilliant, socially sparkling, but again more interested in his career and in success than in justice – indeed finding scruple a rather odd and embarrassing foible. Though his prestige as Attorney-General is significant, however, we see him here in an essentially private role rather than in a political one. For Law Officers seen in their political context, we can look at Attorney-General Sir Gregory Grogram, and Solicitor-General Sir Timothy Beeswax, in *The Prime Minister*.

As John Halperin says, 'Sir Timothy Beeswax, in a sense Daubeny [Disraeli] writ large, is Trollope's final and most devastating metaphor for the totally partisan animal – and the final degradation of the House of Commons. No man more unlike the Duke of Omnium could be imagined.'[37] As a picture of the lawyer-politician on the make, Sir Timothy makes Sir Abraham Haphazard look relatively benign, and Sir Gregory Grogram patient. In *The Prime Minister*, a coalition government is put together, for which the Duke of Omnium is chosen to be Prime Minister. With two parties sharing out the plums, manoeuvring is earnest and intricate among the small fry, but relatively calm among the eminent. 'Noblesse oblige': they felt 'that it behoved them to assume a virtue if they had it not' (I, 76). They take the positions offered.

And Sir Gregory Grogram said not a word, whatever he may have thought, when he was told that Mr. Daubeny's Lord Chancellor, Lord Ramsden, was to keep the seals. Sir Gregory did, no doubt, think very much about it; for legal offices have a signification differing much from that which attaches itself to places simply political. A Lord Chancellor becomes a peer, and on going out of office enjoys a large pension. When the woolsack has been reached there comes an end of doubt, and a beginning of ease. Sir Gregory was not a young man, and this was a terrible blow. But he bore it manfully, saying not a word when the Duke spoke to him; but he became convinced from that moment that no more inefficient lawyer ever sat upon the English bench, or a more presumptuous politician in the British Parliament, than Lord Ramsden. (I, 77)

Sir Gregory and Sir Timothy are yoked together as Attorney-General and Solicitor-General, but their party differences (Sir Gregory Liberal; Sir Timothy Conservative) are not all that separate them. Sir Timothy is calculating, vindictive and resentful on a larger scale, and the frustration of his personal ambitions causes him to play a significant part in the eventual breakdown of the Duke's ministry.

> Then there arose a legal difficulty, which caused much trouble to the coalition Ministry. There fell vacant a certain seat on the bench of judges, – a seat of considerable dignity and importance, but not quite of the highest rank. Sir Gregory Grogram, who was a rich, energetic man, determined to have a peerage, and convinced that, should the coalition fall to pieces, the Liberal element would be in the ascendant, – so that the woolsack would then be open to him, – declined to occupy the place. Sir Timothy Beeswax, the Solicitor-General, saw that it was exactly suited for him, and had no hesitation in expressing his opinion to that effect. But the place was not given to Sir Timothy. It was explained to Sir Timothy that the old rule, – or rather custom, – of offering certain high positions to the law officers of the Crown had been abrogated. Some Prime Minister, or, more probably, some collection of Cabinet Ministers, had asserted the custom to be a bad one, – and, as far as right went, Sir Timothy was declared not to have a leg to stand upon. . . . The Solicitor-General resigned in a huff, and then withdrew his resignation. Sir Gregory thought the withdrawal should not be accepted, having found Sir Timothy to be an unsympathetic colleague. Our Duke consulted the old Duke, among whose theories of official life forbearance to all colleagues and subordinates was conspicuous. The withdrawal was, therefore, allowed, – but the Coalition could not after that be said to be strong in regard to its Law Officers. (I, 134–5)

Trollope's account of this legal and political manoeuvring, with its blend of personal, professional and political strands, is convincing, and it matches the actual rivalries and jockeying for position one finds, for example, in the careers of such eminent legal figures as Lord John Campbell (1779–1861) and Alexander Cockburn (1802–80).[38] 'Some Prime Minister' was Gladstone, and an explanation of the sort sent to Sir Timothy was sent to Trollope's friend, Sir Henry James, upon his appointment as Attorney-General. Says Duman:

> In conformity with the wave of earnestness that influenced the distribution of legal patronage between the mid-1860s and the mid-1880s, Gladstone tried to eliminate the practice of granting the law officers of the crown an almost inalienable right to succeed to senior judicial offices. In 1874 Lord Selborne explained the Prime Minister's policy:
>
>> What Mr.Gladstone did, in the appointment of James and Harcourt, was, to state to them in writing . . . that the offices of A.G. and S.G. if accepted by them, must be accepted on the distinct understanding that they were not accompanied by any title to claim the succession to any Judicial office, on the footing either of any former usage or otherwise.
>
> Nevertheless, even after 1874 the law officers almost invariably ended their legal careers as judges.[39]

Sir Timothy, thus, feels resentment, and his resentment festers within the Coalition. 'It was quite understood that Sir Timothy was inimical to the Coalition though he still belonged to it, and that he would assist in breaking it up if only there were a fair chance of his belonging to the party which would remain in power. Sir Timothy had been badly treated, and did not forget it' (I, 221). Nor is he pleased with Sir Gregory: 'Some by this time hardly coalesced at all, as was the case with Sir Gregory Grogram and Sir Timothy Beeswax' (I, 439). When the scurrilous newspaperman, Slide, accuses the Prime Minister, in the *People's Banner*, of paying Lopez's election expenses and then of hounding 'that poor man to his death in revenge for the trifling sum of money which he was called upon to pay for him' (II, 249), Sir Timothy opposes Sir Gregory's opinions about suing for libel simply because they are Sir Gregory's. As the Coalition weakens, Sir Timothy takes the occasion of the Duke's trying to push through a risky bill to resign in opposition to it, and to attack it in the House. Laurence Fitzgibbon indulges in a very audible whisper: 'The whisper suggested that falling houses were often left by certain animals' (II, 377).

Upon the Duke's fall, Sir Timothy becomes Attorney-General in the new Liberal government and Sir Gregory, whose calculations have been exact, becomes Lord Chancellor. In *The Duke's Children*, Sir Timothy continues his scheming career as Tory leader of the House, using his professional gifts of ornate, glib rhetoric and assumed emotion, 'never stronger than when he simulated anger. His mock indignation was perhaps his most powerful weapon' (I, 245). It is a disillusioned and caustic view of both politics and place-seeking lawyers that Trollope gives us in *The Duke's Children*. The political advocate's indifference to truth, an attitude Trollope regretted in Cicero, but made some excuse for – that Cicero had inherited the sophistical tradition, that he was not a Christian – is here portrayed as sordid. And the Duke's vision of the ideal career as that of 'barristers who are in large practice and also in Parliament', seems the more ironic against such a background.

In fact even the Duke's own idealism is somewhat muted by its immediate context. It is the energetic talk of a father to his exasperatingly listless sons who, out of duty to 'the governor', make a special pact to put in an appearance at breakfast. His selfless work-ethic would perhaps be as removed from what most lawyers would feel as it is to his patient offspring, whose thoughts turn more readily to the bear garden than to the public service.

As I began this section with the Duke's high notion of the law and politics, it is perhaps appropriate to conclude with another of his paternal sermons, this time on the limitations of the law. Chiding young Silverbridge about his proposed marriage to Isabel Boncassen, he asks if Silverbridge has the same freedom to marry as 'the lad out there who is sweeping the walks':

'I suppose I have, – by law.'
'Do you recognise no duty but what the laws impose upon you? Should you be disposed to eat and drink in bestial excess, because the laws would not hinder you? Should you

lie and sleep all day, the law would say nothing! Should you
neglect every duty which your position imposes on you, the
law could not interfere! To such a one as you the law can be
no guide. You should so live as not to come near the law, —
or to have the law to come near to you. From all evil against
which the law bars you, you should be barred, at an infinite
distance by honour, by conscience, and nobility. Does the
law require patriotism, philanthropy, self-abnegation, public service, purity of purpose, devotion to the needs of
others who have been placed in the world below you? The
law is a great thing, — because men are poor and weak, and
bad. And it is great, because where it exists in its strength,
no tyrant can be above it. But between you and me there
should be no mention of law as the guide of conduct. Speak
to me of honour, of duty, and of nobility; and tell me what
they require of you.   (II, 199–200)

Still, neither is this the final word. The governor comes
around. From the man whom Trollope presents, in many
ways if not all, as an ideal politician, however, this carefully
qualified offsetting of law and conscience is significant. The
law, though a great thing, is no more divine than the lawyers.
The lawyer politicians we have examined in the higher
reaches of the law, like Trollope's clergyman, have their
decidedly human failings. What the Duke is describing is two
systems of regulation, an external one by which society is
governed, and the other an internal one, more finely tuned
and adjusted, the voice of tact, discrimination, conscience.
Clearly a lawyer may be a professional in the one without very
strongly registering the other. But our survey of Law Officers
is not yet complete. The most interesting of the lot is Sir
William Patterson, Solicitor-General in *Lady Anna*, who
sounds quite a different note.

6 *Lady Anna*: The Solicitor-General as Prospero

Lady Anna is about legitimacy – the legitimacy of a marriage, the legitimacy of a birth. But beyond these questions of legal fact, it is about legitimacy in a more general and metaphorical sense. At the level of fact, if the Countess Lovel is truly Earl Lovel's wife, her daughter has the right to be called Lady Anna (thus the significance of the title), to be accorded the status and observances due to her rank, and to be capable of inheritance. For, says Blackstone, 'The incapacity of a bastard consists principally in this, that he cannot be heir to any one, neither can he have heirs, but of his own body; for, being *nullius filius*, he is therefore of kin to nobody, and has no ancestor from whom any inheritable blood can be derived.'[1] These are matters of great social and emotional consequence. Though the Countess comes from a humble but respectable background – her father, Captain Murray, 'had come of the right Murrays' (3) – and we have little doubt of her moral status; nevertheless, the establishment of legal fact one way or the other will result in social exaltation or penury. Reflecting on these possibilities, we come to the metaphorical sense of legitimacy, the sense in which we speak of legitimate theatre or legitimate argument;[2] that is, something having a generally recognised status or admissibility. As we have seen, Trollope, on the whole, assents to an inherent social order or fitness of things. His displeasure with the law is usually that it departs from this order, from basic principles of truth and justice, what Bentham would, somewhat sneeringly, have called natural law. 'Legitimacy' thus raises questions not just of factual accuracy and completeness in a given case but of consonance or discrepancy between what satisfies the law and what ought

119

to, what is and what ought to be. The Countess Lovel becomes increasingly obsessed with having them all coincide: her moral conviction, the law's confirmation, and society's regard.

Lady Anna is not singular among Trollope's novels in its preoccupation with the various dimensions of legitimacy, nor is Trollope's treatment of the theme unheralded. The most famous and profound treatment of the subject in English is, perhaps, in *King Lear*. 'Fine word, "legitimate"!' says Edmund in his spirited sardonic speech, 'Now, gods, stand up for bastards!' (I, ii, 1–22), a speech which puts in tension natural, moral, legal and social standards of value. Trollope's *Ralph the Heir*, though with a very different sort of character, poses similar conundrums. The illegitimate Ralph's native benignity and his concern for the estate and its tenants would seem to argue his greater natural appropriateness as heir. But the tenants, even acknowledging his virtues, do not think so. And Trollope sees to it that the feckless but legitimate heir inherits, the social fabric remains untorn, and the 'eternal fitness of things' is asserted. *Ralph* was published in the year *Lady Anna* was written. Seven years later, Trollope returned to the theme of legitimacy in *Is He Popenjoy?* (1877–8), the beginning of which shows a striking resemblance to the beginning of *Lady Anna*. In both an obnoxious aristocrat neglects his land, abuses his family, prefers life in Italy, and returns to England with an Italian woman who he claims is his wife, casting out the rest of the family, and, by a question of legitimacy (in *Popenjoy*, that of the aristocrat's son by the Italian woman), threatening to displace the proper succession. As an accident sets the order of things straight in *Ralph*, so the child's death in Italy restores the right order in *Popenjoy*. At the end of his life, Trollope returned to this complex of issues in *Mr Scarborough's Family*, where we once again have an old man cocking a snook at the law, and playing an extraordinary game of ducks and drakes with the legitimacy of his sons. *Lady Anna*, then, exploits a major Trollopian theme, and, as P. D. Edwards says, though it is 'one of the least known and most friendless of Trollope's novels,' it is also, 'among the more interesting and . . . the more accomplished.'[3]

The novel intricately interlaces law and status. In *An Autobiography*, Trollope dwells retrospectively on *Lady Anna*'s antagonisms of class:

in it a young girl, who is really a lady of high rank and great
wealth, though in her youth she enjoyed none of the privileges of wealth or rank, marries a tailor who had been good
to her, and whom she had loved when she was poor and
neglected . . . everybody found fault with me for marrying
her to the tailor.   (347)

When the novel was in prospect, however, presumably before
that trip to Australia in 1871 when Trollope wrote the novel
on shipboard, he worked out much of the plot in terms of its
legal intricacies and terminology. Just as he had consulted
Charles Merewether on the law of heirlooms and widows'
paraphernalia for *The Eustace Diamonds* (which he left with the
Fortnightly Review before embarking for Australia), so he consulted again about the legalities of *Lady Anna*. This time,
however, the legal questions involve much more of the novel's
plot. The consultation survives on the front and back of an
unsigned sheet of paper among the Trollope Papers[4] in the
Bodleian Library. It is an interesting document, showing
Trollope thinking out his story as a series of legal complications. It also shows once again his concern for accuracy. He
outlines the legal groundwork of his plot and asks questions in
the left-hand column, and his consultant responds on the
right.

Lord A makes a fictitious marriage
with Miss B, and afterwards marries
Miss C.
He then repudiates C on the ground
that she is not his wife he having
been a married man when he
pretended to marry her.

a ~~prosecution~~ C ~~procures that an action~~ for bigamy	Wrong phraseology should be C institutes a prosecution for bigamy
~~????~~ is ~~brought~~; but A is acquitted because the first marriage is not proved. C again claims to be the wife; but by this time – A is in a madhouse, and ~~???~~ and C's claim is disputed by D the distant heir. D says that though the first marriage was not proved at the bigamy trial, it was not disproved He is able to shew that A+B were received as man and wife	This is quite right – The acquittal is no estoppel agst D – he may show the real truth [e.g.?] prior marriage by A.

A dies mad, and D inherits
the title. C claims property on
behalf of her daughter and
ultimately succeeds.

Would it rest with C to prove that the first marriage was no marriage, or with D to prove that it was?	With D to prove it was a marriage. C would prove her own marriage – which prima facie proves her to be A's wife. D must then show that altho' a de facto marriage between A and C it is invalid on account of prior marriage of A
Would the aquittal on the charge of bigamy be taken as ~~see~~ proof that the ~~first~~ marriage was void?	It would be evidence – but not conclusive – as I have said the real facts may be shown but if a question of fact has to be determined by a Jury the fact of the acquittal ~~be~~ would be placed before them as an incident in the case – but other proof of the real state of fact could be pressed.
If there be any legal inconsistency in my story could you point it out.	No inconsistencies at all.

Besides settling minor questions of terminology (whether one procures, brings or institutes an action or a prosecution for bigamy), the questions and answers establish correct procedures for proving the legitimacy of a marriage and of property rights in a complicated situation involving several parties with various interests. In the novel itself, Trollope probes the hopes and tactics of all these parties, including their many lawyers, and provides many technical summaries of the litigation. Clearly for him, as for the socially-interested reader, the legal niceties of the plot, like the philosophical stepping stones of a theodicy or the disputations of *Paradise Lost*, are an essential part of the novel's intellectual play and satisfaction. They explore and display the ritual structures of social cohesion and exclusion. Earl Lovel, with his Italianate corruption and defiance of English decorum, creates social chaos: 'marriage and blood relationship as established by all laws since the days of Moses, were odious to him and ridiculous in his sight, because all obligations were distasteful to him, – and all laws, except those which preserved to him the use of his own money' (14).

As the Countess Lovel, fighting for her legitimate social status, dominates the novel's class drama, Sir William Patterson, the Solicitor-General, dominates its legal drama. As James Kincaid says, 'They divide the novel between them.'[5] Sir William, however, is especially interesting. Enigmatic, humane, and exasperating to his fellow professionals, he presides over the action like a tutelary spirit.

A preliminary outline of the book in its legal dimensions will help. With no fortune or settlement, Josephine Murray marries Earl Lovel, a nobleman from the vicinity of Keswick in the Lake District of northern England. Within six months he tells her their marriage is illegitimate, he being already married to an Italian woman. He is clearly a scoundrel and a lecher. He returns to Italy, and she gives birth to their daughter, Anna. After five years, the Countess institutes a prosecution for bigamy, but the Earl is acquitted, the Italian marriage not being proved. Cast off, and with little money, the Countess receives support from a Keswick tailor and his son. Lovel eventually turns up again with a new Italian woman, Signorina Spondi, but is much aged, rumoured to be mad, and soon dies: 'The life which he had led no doubt had had its allurments, but it is one which hardly admits of a hale and happy evening. Men who make women a prey, prey also on themselves' (12). His will bequeaths his property to Signorina Spondi, except for the meagre amount of entailed land which goes with his title to a distant heir, Frederic Lovel. Among his other un-English activities, the old Earl 'had sold estates in other counties, converting unentailed acres into increased wealth, but wealth of a kind much less acceptable to the general English aristocrat than that which comes direct from the land' (3). His personal property, therefore, 'in shares and funds and ventures of commercial speculation here and there, after the fashion of tradesmen' (303), is very large. And since personal property does not go with the entail, the heir to the estate will get little but the status of calling himself an earl. Setting aside the will on the grounds that the Earl was mad when he made it will dispose of Signorina Spondi, but what happens then is still quite complicatedly in doubt. Trollope clearly feels that the reader needs help in appreciating the intricacy of the situation, and writes the following guide to the net of interlacing interests:

The young Earl clearly inherited the title and the small estate at Lovel Grange. The Italian woman was prima facie heiress to everything else, – except to such portion of the large personal property as the widow could claim as widow, in the event of her being able to prove that she had been a wife. But in the event of the will being no will, the Italian woman would have nothing. In such case the male heir would have all if the marriage were no marriage; – but would have nothing if the marriage could be made good. If the marriage could be made good, the Lady Anna would have the entire property, except such portion as would be claimed of right by her mother, the widow. Thus the Italian woman and the young lord were combined in interest against the mother and daughter as regarded the marriage; and the young lord and the mother and daughter were combined against the Italian woman as regarded the will; – but the young lord had to act alone against the Italian woman, and against the mother and daughter whom he and his friends regarded as swindlers and imposters. It was for him to set aside the will in reference to the Italian woman, and then to stand the brunt of the assault made upon him by the soi-distant wife.　(17–18)

What interests Trollope in this farrago of litigation is the notion of social authentication. The Countess hopes the bigamy trial will establish her status: 'if he were acquitted, then would her claim to be called Lady Lovel, and enjoy the appanages of her rank, be substantiated' (8). He *is* acquitted – but her rank is not substantiated. 'It was, of course, her object that all the world should acknowledge her to be the Countess Lovel, and her daughter to be the Lady Anna. But all the world could not be made to do this by course of law' (11). Public opinion, in fact, runs the gamut: she was reckless in marriage; she really knew about the other marriage; she lives with a mere tailor who assaulted her husband; 'she drank'. Among the tales about her:

Others were reported which had in them some grains of truth, – as that she was violent, stiff-necked, and vindictive. Had they said of her that it had become her one religion to assert her daughter's right, – per fas aut nefas, – to assert it

by right or wrong; to do justice to her child let what injustice
might be done to herself or others, – then the truth would
have been spoken.   (9)

Truth, authenticity, the bubble reputation, are not so easily
held fast. Reality versus public opinion, legality versus justice,
principle versus fanaticism – the social ambiguities multiply.
The bigamy trial itself is very much a gamble: 'Should she
succeed [that is, make good her charge of bigamy], she would
be a penniless, unmarried female with a daughter, her child
would be unfathered and base' (8). And the result is nebulous,
the Earl's hypothetical earlier marriage neither proved nor
disproved. After his death, when inheritance is the issue,
indecisiveness again prevails, only niggardly amounts being
provided from the estate to help the Countess prove her
claim.

As we have seen, Trollope also presents these ambiguities of
identity and status in terms of class. Mulling over the rights of
inheritence, social imagination swerves towards the young
Earl:

It would be better for the English world that the young Earl
should be a rich man, fit to do honour to his position, fit to
marry the daughter of a duke, fit to carry on the glory of the
English peerage, than that a woman, ill-reputed in the
world, should be established as a Countess, with a daughter
dowered with tens of thousands, as to whom it was already
said that she was in love with a tailor's son.   (21)

Though we might expect Trollope to side with 'the English
world', he characteristically creates a moral tension, the duties
of class balanced against personal honour concerning a promise given. The issues are nicely adjusted by Lady Anna
defending Daniel to Miss Bluestone:

'I will tell you the truth, dear. I am ashamed to marry Mr.
Thwaite, – not for myself, but because I am Lord Lovel's
cousin and mamma's daughter. And I should be ashamed
to marry Lord Lovel.'
    'Why, dear?'
    'Because I should be false and ungrateful.'   (234)

Anna is moved by 'the unutterable sweetness of the young
Earl' (132). And the narrator hardly epouses Daniel's Jacobin
principles. Of Daniel's class antagonism on hearing from Sir
William Patterson that the 'titles of nobility are in England the
outward emblem of noble conduct', the narrator writes: 'With
his half-knowledge, his ill-gotten and ill-digested information, with his reading which had all been on one side, he had
been unable as yet to catch a glimpse of the fact that from the
ranks of the nobility are taken the greater proportion of the
hard-working servants of the State' (305–6). But the matter is
not at all one-sided. 'He is clever, and can talk about things
better than my cousin.' says Anna (234). And the narrator
allows some ironic ambiguity. When Miss Bluestone pronounces: 'I think that a girl who is a lady, should never marry a
man who is not a gentleman,' the narrator concludes, 'So
spoke the young female Conservative with wisdom beyond
her years' (234–5). Many of Trollope's readers seem to have
sided with Miss Bluestone. In *An Autobiography*, Trollope says
of Lady Anna's marrying Daniel:

> It was my wish of course to justify her in doing so, and to
> carry my readers along with me in my sympathy with her.
> But everybody found fault with me for marrying her to the
> tailor. What would they have said if I had allowed her to jilt
> the tailor and marry the good-looking young lord? How
> much louder, then, would have been the censure!   (347)

Answering a complaint from Lady Wood, he chose to stick
with irony: 'It is very dreadful, but there was no other way.'[6]
    To the anxieties about outward authentication, legitimacy
and status that the book raises, Trollope, in other words, poses
a familiar Romantic response, that suggested by Burns's

> The rank is but the guinea's stamp
> The Man's the gowd for a' that.

P. D. Edwards notes that by setting the novel unusually far
back in the past, starting in the second decade of the century
and in the Lake District, Trollope gives his 'worse-than-
Byronic villain',[7] Earl Lovel, an appropriate era. But the

political connotations are also appropriate. The radical Thwaites are acquaintances of the 'poets of the lakes, who had not as yet become altogether Tories' (33). (Everyone would recall Jeffrey's famous attacks on them in the *Edinburgh Review* as 'opposed to all existing authority', and 'waging a desperate war on the established system of public taste and judgement.'[8] Trollope may not go as far as Burns in thinking 'A man's a man for a' that', but he does, for all the rough edges he gives to Daniel, present him with considerable sympathy, making him forbearing even when shot by the distraught Countess Lovel.[9] And he attributes to him some characteristically chauvinistic Trollopian notions about marriage and property: '"I don't want my wife to have anything of her own before marriage, . . . but she certainly shall have nothing after marriage, – independent of me." For a man with sound views of domestic power and marital rights always choose a Radical!' (483). In any case, Lady Anna makes her eventual decision on the basis of Daniel's personal worth and her promise to him.

The two chief figures of the novel beyond the amatory plot are the Countess and Sir William Patterson, the Solicitor-General. The Countess is another Trollopian study in obsession. She is the victim of injustice, but the long grim struggle to establish her rights turns her into a fanatic, and 'she expected that her daughter would be ambitious, as she was ambitious' (80). Though the Thwaites have supported her at great sacrifice in her long contest, Daniel's status as a tradesman suitor disgusts her. She wants the debt to the Thwaites paid 'if only that she might be able to treat the man altogether as an enemy' (314). In the end she is ready to kill to have her notions of rank fulfilled in her daughter's marriage. She expresses herself in melodramatic clichés: 'Would it not be better that she [Anna] should die?' (395); and 'If this is to go on, . . . one of us must die' (412). Edwards again notes perceptively that her theatrical language is essentially manipulative, an attempt to give tragic status to resistant reality: 'To this extent, the worst tragedy for many of Trollope's more passionate characters . . . is the impossibility of tragedy.' And he points to her curious collapse into mundane personal concern after her attempt at murder: 'The feelings that prompted her criminal act, feelings that had held sway over her for more than a year, do not outlive the act itself by even a few minutes. She must live with the bathetic truth that her own life is after all more valuable to her than her family honour.'[10] The notions of class and fitness that Trollope might approve in another context have become, in the Countess, ossified, insensitive and stagey.

The emotional effect of *Lady Anna* is controlled by its two contrasting motifs of obsession and accommodation. Trollope is good at representing obsession – as in the grim and pro-longed disintegration of Louis Trevelyan in *He Knew He Was Right*. What starts as a commendable determination to resist her husband's abuse and assert her just status becomes more and more hard-edged as the Countess fights for it year after year. The long battle for her version of paradise turns her life into a desert filled with contending predators. The contrasting motif of accommodation, and perhaps the novel as a whole, is dominated by Sir William Patterson, who enters the novel very much as though he were going to be the epitome of Trollope's savage barristers. At the very idea of compromise (that is, of a convenient marriage between Anna and the young Earl), 'Sir William Patterson stood aghast and was dismayed. Sir William intended to make mincemeat of the Countess. It was said of him that he intended to cross-examine the Countess off her legs, right out of her claim, and almost into her grave' (23). But he soon changes into a sort of benign, legal deity ruling over the novel. His role is rather like that of Prospero in *The Tempest* or, though more pleasantly, of the Duke in *Measure for Measure*; an *architectus* as Frye would say, controlling a type of 'comic action established by Aristopha-nes'. Here as there, 'an older man, instead of retiring from the action, builds it up on the stage.'[11]

One does not often think of Trollope in these terms. Critics have dwelt rather heavily on Trollope's realism, his 'complete appreciation of the usual', as Henry James put it. [12] But the novel, particularly as descended from Trollope's admired Thackeray, characteristically plays upon the tension between realism and romance. The archetypal elements of Greek New Comedy as Frye describes them[13] are strikingly present in *Lady Anna*. The obstructive, wintry society of elders, restrictive social forms, and pettyfogging lawyers oppressing the young lovers is evident. And the triumph of the lovers in a ritual marriage that sets things right is also clear. 'The movement from *pistis* to *gnosis*, from a society controlled by habit, ritual bondage, arbitrary law and the older characters to a society controlled by youth and pragmatic freedom,' says Frye, 'is fundamentally, as the Greek words suggest, a movement from illusion to reality. Illusion is whatever is fixed or definable, and reality is best understood as its negation: whatever reality is, it's not *that*. Hence the importance of the theme of creating and dispelling illusion in comedy: the illusions caused by disguise, obsession, hypocrisy, or unknown parentage.'[14] With his unfailing capacity for questioning institutions he believes in, Trollope shows his hierarchical society as capable of tending to a set of rigid prescriptions and prejudices: those of the obsessive Countess, of the 'violent Tory' clergyman, Charles Lovel (51), of the ferociously partisan lawyers, of malicious public opinion. And he comes to a characteristically temperate conclusion. Lady Anna marries her tailor, but having reached a generous accommodation with his rival, the young Earl, who gets half her fortune. And there are suggestions that the tailor, too, can be assimilated, as a clubman, a member of parliament, and a 'wiser man' (401, 489, 513). The moral of the comedy structure is the same as that Burke applied to states: a society 'without the means of some change is without the means of its conservation.'[15]

Most interesting in this pattern is that the master of generosity, vitality and accommodation is found among the customary forces of prescription and formality, in the office of the Solicitor-General. Sir William has the appropriate qualities of a magisterial *architectus*, disquietingly so to his colleagues. He has 'the gift of seeing through darkness' (46). And instead of confining himself to one camp, he bestrides the whole field, shocking his more conventional colleagues on both sides by dining with contending parties and holding meetings of the opposing sets of lawyers. He enrages Bluestone by giving advice to Bluestone's clients. While other lawyers are champions of the *idée fixe*, and the exclusive right of their clients, Sir William looks amicably to creative compromise. Initially, when the young Earl has the title and the real estate and Anna seems to have a claim to the money, Patterson thinks it fitting that they should marry. Later, he goes beyond abandoning the exclusive claims of his client and promotes the marriage of Lady Anna and Daniel. Like the lawyers the clergyman, Charles Lovel, is scandalised, believing in the tradition of

Lord Brougham 'that an English barrister would be true to his client' (326).

The resulting trial, 'Lovel versus Murray and Another,' to determine who should inherit the old Earl's personal property is accordingly very peculiar. Sir William gives an eloquent address, bearing out his intention 'to state a case as much in the interest of my opponents as of my clients' (292). He generously denies any doubt of the Countess's marital status. In effect, he withdraws his claim; but since the Italian woman may still press hers, he wishes the case to continue so that the matter may be cleared up once and for all. As to the opposing counsel for the Countess, Sir William says, 'there is no reason why my learned friend and I should not sit together, having our briefs and our evidence in common' (296). All this is scandalous to his juniors and to the Bar in general. From almost the beginning, 'Sir William was anxious to settle the thing comfortably for all parties. Mr. Hardy [also for the Earl] was determined not only that right should be done, but also that it should be done in a righteous manner' (64). For the Countess, Serjeant Bluestone, 'a very violent man, taking up all his cases as though the very holding of a brief opposite to him was an insult to himself' (48), is equally given to vehemence and indignation: 'It is just like Patterson, who always thinks he can make laws according to the light of his own reason' (87). Charles Lovel calls Sir William 'this apostate barrister' (303). And the Bar in general agrees

> that the Solicitor-General had done badly for his client. The sum of money which was at stake was, they said, too large to be played with. As the advocate of the Earl, Sir William ought to have kept himself aloof from the Countess and her daughter. In lieu of regarding his client, he had taken upon himself to set things right in general, according to his idea of right. No doubt he was a clever man, and knew how to address a jury, but he was always thinking of himself, and bolstering up something of his own, instead of thinking of his case and bolstering up his client. (323)

The opinion of the Attorney-General is carefully qualified, balancing praise and blame in the same judgement: '"He is a great man, – a very great man indeed," said the Attorney-

General, in answer to someone who was abusing Sir William. "There is not one of us who can hold a candle to him. But, then, as I have always said, he ought to have been a poet!'" (348). The complaints of his colleagues, that he appeals to 'the light of his own reason', to 'his idea of right', to 'something of his own', indicate that, unlike most Trollopian lawyers, and in accord with Trollope's ideals, he consults an inner light of truth. The criticism that he should have been a poet draws attention not only to his creative imagination but to his role as *architectus*, as maker.

Sir William is the spokesman of romance in its opposition to the obstructive, disintegrative society. Though he initially considers that the marriage of Lady Anna to Daniel would be 'a grievous injury to the social world of his country' (204), he comes around to promoting it.

> Gentlemen, you have no romance among you,' said Sir William. 'Have not generosity and valour always prevailed over wealth and rank with ladies in story?'
>
> 'I do not remember any valorous tailors who have succeeded with ladies of high degree,' said Mr. Hardy.
>
> 'Did not the lady of the Strachey marry the yeoman of the wardrobe?' asked the Solicitor-General.
>
> 'I don't know that we care much about romance here,' said the Serjeant.   (318)

As well as alluding to Malvolio's hopeful line from *Twelfth Night*, (II, v, 35–6), Sir William might have mentioned Grimm's 'The Valiant Little Tailor' – the phenomenon is not unknown. But Hardy draws the line of social imagination clearly. And after the trial, 'There was a feeling that the Solicitor-General had been carried away by some romantic idea of abstract right, and had acted in direct opposition to all the usages of forensic advocacy as established in England' (348).

It is finally appropriate to his special role in the novel that, when Daniel Thwaite is becoming 'silent and almost morose' under the social burdens of his marriage, Sir William saves the day by making a speech that touches both on the pleasure of all concerned that the bride's rights and rank have been recognised and on Daniel's devotion and constancy. His speech harmonises the occasion. 'The hero of the day was the

Solicitor-General' (507). And the novel ends on a note of accommodation, reintegration of class, combination in marriage, and the resurgence of life.

In creating Sir William, Trollope might seem at first to have reversed his general assumptions about lawyers. But it is clear that he thinks of Sir William as exceptional – thus all the criticism from the other lawyers in the book – and that he presents him as what a lawyer ought to be. Where the others are partial, and savage, he is interested in the welfare of all concerned. Where they are mechanical and convention-bound, he exercises imagination. Where they consult only their client's cause, he consults his inner light of truth. Where their notion of truth is self-righteous, his is humane. And he is geniality itself, temperamentally most unlike Trollope, though he possesses the virtues Trollope considers essential to the best social and professional life: 'Sir William Patterson was a gentleman as well as a lawyer; – one who had not simply risen to legal rank by diligence and intellect, but a gentleman born and bred, who had been at a public school, and had lived all his days with people of the right sort'(183). It is interesting to compare his professional style with that of Chaffanbrass. Trollope spoke condescendingly of Chaffanbrass as cock of the Old Bailey dunghill. He uses the same rhetorical figure for Sir William in the Court of Queen's Bench, but very much tempered:

It is always satisfactory to see the assurance of a cock crowing in his own farmyard, and to admire his easy familiarity with things that are awful to a stranger bird. If you, O reader, or I were bound to stand up in that court, dressed in wig and gown, and to tell a story that would take six hours in the telling, the one or the other of us knowing it to be his special duty so to tell it that judge, and counsellors, and jury, should all catch clearly every point that was to be made, – how ill would that story be told, how would those points escape the memory of the teller, and never come near the intellect of the hearers. . . . But our Solicitor-General rose to his legs a happy man, with all that grace of motion, that easy slowness, that unassumed confidence which always belongs to the ordinary doings of our familiar life.   (291–2)

It is as though Trollope had closed his Carlyle and opened his Arnold. His account of Sir William in action is amused but full of admiration. Henry Drinker suggests that Sir William's wisdom, suavity and force of character may owe much to 'the polished, good-humoured, powerful and successful barristers whom Trollope met at the Garrick and Athenaeum', and the idea is plausible.[16]

Trollope suggests that the very qualities that make Sir William an enigma and a trial of patience to other lawyers are also what place him on a special level of achievement. By comparison, Mr Hardy, for example, 'hated compromise and desired justice, – and was a great rather than a successful lawyer' (46). While this suggests something admirable about Mr Hardy, of course, the conclusion to be drawn is not that Sir William is merely successful. He is both – great and successful as well. His handling of 'Lovel versus Murray and Another', nevertheless, gives rise to considerable speculation about political consequences for his career. 'Many thought that he had altogether cut his own throat, and that he would have to take the first 'puny' judgeship vacant' (348). On the other hand, if accommodations could be made, 'If the Earl could get even five thousand a year out of the property, it was thought that the Solicitor-General might hold his own and in due time become at any rate a Chief Baron' (349).

While a Victorian reader familiar with the typical career patterns of the Law Officers of the Crown might follow this easily, a modern reader, especially a modern American reader acquainted with a different system, might be somewhat at a loss. Let me give a thumbnail sketch. The Prime Minister appoints the Solicitor-General, who is normally knighted. He is nearly always an MP, frequently a Privy Councillor, but not normally a member of the Cabinet. He often succeeds to the office of Attorney-General, then to a judicial appointment (possibly even to the Lord Chancellorship). In the passages quoted eventual judicial appointments for Sir William are in question. At the time of *Lady Anna* (1873), the plums would be appointment as Lord Chief Justice, or as a Chief Justice of the Court of Queen's Bench or Court of Common Pleas, or as a Chief Baron of the Court of Exchequer,[17] depending, of course, upon vacancies. A puisne ('puny') judge – the most Sir

William can now hope to be in the view of the gossipers – is a superior-court judge inferior in rank to the Chief Justices. Trollope has it all straight, and the political interest about Sir William's involvement in and conduct of the case adds, with all the niceties of calculation, a socially realistic note to the otherwise romantic role he performs.

If the pattern of New Comedy gives a special interest to this drama of legitimacy, status and social order, we must nevertheless recognise that it is a pattern modified in appropriately Trollopian directions. The result is not simply triumph over obstructive forces but accommodation. The lawyers, however restive, are persuaded to comply. Lady Anna gains her property, but she gives half of it to the Earl – thus accommodating the view of 'the English world that the young Earl should be a rich man, fit to do honour to his position' (21). The *architectus* is a public school man with a reverence for the social hierarchy who lives among 'people of the right sort'. In fact, Sir William overcomes not only external discord but some of his own inclinations. On a first view, he had been ready 'to make mincemeat of the Countess', just as he later, on hearing of Lady Anna's lowly attachment, thinks 'the marriage of Lady Anna Lovel, with a colossal fortune, to Daniel Thwaite the tailor, would be a grievous injury to the social world of his country' (204). But his capacity for sympathetic projection brings him to accommodation. Like Burke's statesman who 'always considers how he shall make the most of the existing materials of his country',[18] he instinctively moves toward creative concord. Daniel is rough material, but Sir William comforts him and the novel ends with the hint of how Daniel 'became perhaps a wiser man' (513).

The effect is that grace is added to legitimacy. While maintaining a sceptical view of the ordinary lawyer's disposition to zealotry and discord, Trollope allows, in the figure of Sir William, for a higher notion of law. Though Trollope presents this notion humorously (Sir William 'was a man especially given to make excuses for poor weak, erring, unlearned mortals, ignorant of the law' [205]), it is an essentially charitable, harmonising notion.

7 *Mr. Scarborough's Family*: The Idea of the Law

Even in the context of Trollope's fascination with law and lawyers, the legal machinations and complexities of *Mr. Scarborough's Family*, a posthumously published novel, are remarkable for their range and comprehensiveness. In this novel, also, Trollope's usual intricate combination of social rules and individual perversities is never far removed from fundamental questions about the nature of law itself. Is it a majestic moral structure built to the music of universal principles or is it an instrument to be wielded, this way or that, as personal whim and momentary advantage dictate?

Old Mr Scarborough, Squire of Tretton, an estate enriched by the growth of a town and a pottery works on its land, lies dying by inches under the surgeon's knife. His guardsman son, Mountjoy, has gambled away the inheritance in post-obit debts – debts, that is, to be paid after his father's death when Mountjoy will have inherited. But Scarborough astounds his son and confounds the creditors by announcing that Mountjoy was born before Scarborough married, and that he has the wedding certificate to prove it. The estate therefore, will go to his second son, Augustus. To avoid future harassment, Augustus settles with Mountjoy's creditors for a fraction of their claims, then gloats over his father's approaching death with such indelicate relish that old Scarborough produces a second set of marriage documents, reinstating Mountjoy despite his gambling propensities. In the subplot, Harry Annesley, heir to his uncle, Squire Prosper of Buston, unwisely shows a cavalier distaste for his uncle's pleasure in reading lugubrious sermons to the family, so Prosper determines to marry in vengeance and disinherit Harry by spitefully getting a son to displace him. Mr Grey, of the firm of Grey and Barry, represents both Scarborough and Prosper, thus

tying the two disinheritance plots together. Trollope not only
uses the law to tie the novel's characters together, articulating
their relationships by means of legal contention pursued into
the intricacies of inheritance, entails and marriage settlements,
but also, in exasperated disputes between Scarborough and
Grey over the dignity of the law, raises fundamental questions
about the relationship of law to justice, the things that are
Caesar's and the things that are God's.

Trollope's familiar values – truth, honesty, duty – find their
spokesman in Scarborough's attorney, Mr Grey: 'he certainly
was an honest man, and had taken up the matter [of the
Scarborough inheritance] simply with a view of learning the
truth' (145). Convinced of the majesty and dignity of the law,
he is in the tradition of Grotius and Blackstone, arguing that
the law of the land gives expression to principles of abstract
justice. Blackstone, for example, in his famous *Commentaries
on the Laws of England*, asserts: 'as man depends absolutely
upon his Maker for everything, it is necessary that he should
in all points conform to his Maker's will. This will of his Maker
is called the law of nature . . . no human laws are of any
validity, if contrary to this.'[1] Grey's daughter, Dolly, considers
him superior to his partner, Mr Barry, in being governed by
'considerations as to radical good or evil' (502), what
Blackstone would call natural law (radical good) or '*mala in se*'
(inherent evil). From the earliest times, however, people have
uneasily distinguished between a natural sense of justice derived from God or reason (Blackstone's realm of natural law)
and the laws made by man. The eighteenth century made the
discord acute. As George Sabine observes, David Hume, if
one grants his premises, 'made a clean sweep of the whole
rationalist philosophy of natural right, of self-evident truths,
and of the laws of eternal and immutable morality which were
supposed to guarantee the harmony of nature and the order
of human society.'[2] Through Bentham and Mill, Hume's
scepticism continues its unsettling course into the core of
Victorian thoughts about social regimen.

Unfortunately, Mr Grey has in old Mr Scarborough a client
who 'had lived through his life with the one strong resolution
of setting the law at defiance in reference to the distribution of
his property; but chiefly because he had thought the law to be
unjust' (74). Moreover, to Grey's annoyance and sorrow,

Scarborough, in his legal *legerdemain*, 'cares nothing for truth. He scorns it, and laughs at it' (157). If he had had the opportunity, one might imagine Scarborough wickedly savouring the caustic irony of Jeremy Bentham's extended diatribe, in *A Comment on the Commentaries*, against Blackstone's 'theological grimgribber'. To Blackstone's pious equation of man's law with the law of nature and the will of God, Bentham responds: 'Nothing can be more harmonious than this, were it but intelligible.' But, says Bentham, warming to his task:

> It is the way with lawyers, and above all with this lawyer: They can no more speak at their ease without a fiction in their mouths, than Demosthenes without pebbles. . . . They feed upon untruth, as the Turks do upon opium, at first from choice and with their eyes open, afterwards by habit, till at length they lose all shame, avow it for what it is, and swallow it with greediness, not bearing to be without it.[3]

As for Blackstone's definition of positive or man-made law as 'a rule of civil conduct . . . commanding what is right and prohibiting what is wrong,'[4] Bentham writes scornfully:

> Were I to be asked what it is I mean when I call an action a *right* one, I should answer very readily: neither more nor less than, an action I *approve* of: and so of a *wrong* action, an action I *disapprove* of. . . . *Right* he will tell you . . . is what is commanded by the Law of Nature or . . . the Law of Revelation. *Wrong* what is prohibited by that same or those same laws. . . . 'tis our friend the Law of Nature, only in masquerade, that we are got back again to once more. . . . The bottom of all this is, it is the case with this Author, as it is with me: he does not like bad laws, laws that are wrong, laws in short that he does not like.[5]

Approbation and disapprobation – this is the language and argument of David Hume on the derivation of moral distinctions: 'disapprobation . . . lies in yourself, not in the object. . . . when you pronounce any action or character to be vicious, you mean nothing, but that from the constitution of your nature you have a feeling or sentiment of blame from the contemplation of it.'[6]

The quarrel is how we know and identify what is and is not virtuous. It has been suggested by Michael Timko that the basic concern of Victorian literature is epistemological rather than metaphysical, not how man is related to God, but whether man can know anything about his place in the scheme of things, whether any ultimate sanctions are discoverable.[7] In Mr Scarborough, who adopts a position even more extreme than Bentham's, though with the same zest for deflating pieties, Trollope gives the sceptical attitude full rein, calling in question even his own authorial values. And we note that by the end, Scarborough has been wicked, loved, triumphant while Mr Grey is decent, hoodwinked, self-doubting, super-annuated. 'Law', says Sir Ernest Barker, 'is not ethics; and legality, or obedience to law, is not the same as morality. Law is concerned with external acts. . . . Ethics is concerned not only with external acts, but also with internal motive: its essence, as Aristotle said, is "a state of character, concerned with choice."'[8] Such a cobweb of interests, focussed in a state of character, and with Trollope giving the Devil his due and then some, is the essence of *Mr. Scarborough's Family.*

In addition to the distinction between Caesar's and God's laws, Christian tradition observes a tension between justice and love: 'where justice growes, there grows eke greter grace.'[9] This triple distinction between law, justice and love is evident in Trollope's assessment of Scarborough at his death, underscoring the irony that despite his reputation for wicked-ness, he is motivated by love:

> in every phase of his life he had been actuated by love for others. He had never been selfish, thinking always of others rather than of himself. . . . For the conventionalities of the law he entertained a supreme contempt, but he did wish so to arrange matters with which he was himself concerned as to do what justice demanded.   (567)

It is, of course, for God to choose whether strict justice or love should be dispensed, whether an eye for an eye (one notices in the same obituary that Scarborough 'could hate to distrac-tion') or divine grace, but Scarborough enjoys with marvellous insouciance the power, the inscrutability, and the cleverness of the godly function he assumes. He is a sort of comic version of Job's inscrutable God, Yahweh, with whom Job too tries to reason in forensic language and imagery.[10] Scarborough has a great zest for striking awe into his beholders: "'I am sure he is going to do something very dreadful this time," [Miss Scarborough] whispered to Mr Grey, who seemed himself to be a little awestruck, and did not answer her' (519). Scarborough possesses and manipulates. Fond of people who belong to him, he is ready to marry his son to his niece so that she too 'might be made in part thus to belong to himself' (14). And he affects indifference to moral accusation: 'I care nothing for their judgment' (73). He is not to be circumscribed by conventional expectations: 'he could not undertake to live precisely by rule' (365).

The great difference between Scarborough and Job's untractable God is that Scarborough has a sense of humour: 'He always showed some enjoyment of the fun which arose from the effects of his own scheming' (194). He relishes scandalising decent society as in his contempt for the idea that law is sacred. To Mr Grey, for whom the laws are 'as Holy Writ' (526), Scarborough seems to be something between an atheist and a blasphemer – and more maddeningly still, a complacent one to boot:

> 'He hasn't got a God. He believes only in his own reason, – and is content to do so, lying there on the very brink of eternity. He is quite content with himself. . . . He has no reverence for property and the laws which govern it. . . . It is his utter disregard for law, – for what the law has decided, which makes me declare him to have been the wickedest man the world ever produced. (157)

For his part, Scarborough takes such opinions, whether from Mr Grey, 'who constantly told him to his face that he was a rascal' (195), or from his son Mountjoy, 'quite as a compliment' (393), almost purring with quiet satisfaction:

> '. . . you've done a monstrous injustice to everybody concerned.'
> 'I rather like doing what you call injustices.'
> 'You have set the law at defiance.'
> 'Well; yes; I think I have done that.' (394)

Judging by motive rather than external action, he considers that 'though a man may break the law, he need not therefore be accounted bad, and though he may have views of his own as to religious matters, he need not be an atheist' (202). Nevertheless, the 'law was hardly less absurd to him than religion' (194). Appropriating the language of religion, he thinks the law 'in endeavouring to make arrangements for his property . . . sinned so greatly as to drive a wise man to much scheming' (523). Similarly when, revolted by Augustus's desire to see him dead and out of the way, he revokes the trick that would have let Augustus inherit the estate, he pronounces: 'I think that you have behaved damnably, and that I have punished you' (545).

A fierce hater actuated by love, a defier of law with a sense of justice, affecting indifference to opinion but wounded to the quick by his son's open wish to see him dead, Scarborough is a marvellously complex creation. Though readers have tried to find a special philosophical principle in his devious actions, Booth's statement that 'the subject is property and its influence upon family relationships' strikes me as sound even in its simplicity, for there is something elemental in Scarborough's motivation.[11] Though Trollope says Scarborough 'hated the law, – because it was the law' (188), his hatred stems from an instinct of possession: 'If a man has a property,' says Scarborough, 'he should be able to leave it as he pleases; or, — or else he doesn't have it' (389). He is tolerant of Augustus's greed because, 'There is no such word in the language as enough. An estate can have but one owner here' (74). And he is bemused that Mountjoy should feel aggrieved at news of his illegitimacy, because 'To be illegitimate would be, he thought, nothing unless illegitimacy carried with it loss of property' (6). Though Trollope insists that 'Mr. Scarborough was not a selfish man' (188), Scarborough nevertheless has an irrational attachment to his property as firm and elemental as a barnacle's to a rock. If we think his attitude extreme, however, we should perhaps remember Blackstone's own language as he winds up to discourse on 'The Rights of Things' in his *Commentaries*: 'There is nothing', says Blackstone, 'which so generally strikes the imagination, and engages the affections of mankind, as the right of property; or that sole and despotic dominion which one man claims and exercises over the external things of the world, in total exclusion of the right of any other individual in the universe.'[12]

In his animal possessiveness we touch on another intriguingly ambiguous facet of Scarborough. In many ways he is immensely attractive, enjoying unbounded self satisfaction as well. To the law-abiding mind, he is in his way anarchic, the id triumphant, acknowledging no standard of approbation but his own. Less secure spirits like Mr Grey or the reader are nevertheless fascinated by him. Even his love, which Trollope assures us had actuated him in every phase of his life, is expended on people who 'belong to himself', so that his very love and unselfishness are, in this view, a kind of self-love, just as his leaving property, if he can leave it as he pleases, is paradoxically having it. Readers have noted how far Trollope often goes in appreciating characters at odds with his own values of truth and honesty. Scarborough's attitude to his estate confronts us with such a tension. The elemental, unrestrainable grasp, the closed jaw of the bulldog, the character who will not and cannot let go is, of course, a Trollopian speciality. Lizzie Eustace with her diamonds, 'this selfish, hard-fisted little woman, who could not bring herself to abandon the plunder on which she had laid her hand' (*ED*, 43)[13] is the most dramatic instance. Perhaps Trollope allows Scarborough a larger degree of sympathy in his possessiveness because in the end the affairs of the estate work out according to Trollope's class ideology and sense of English tradition: the elder son, however much a scapegrace, inherits. Still, megalomaniac as Cockshut rightly calls him,[14] there is a difference between Scarborough, whose identification with his property allows him to give of himself in it, and his son Augustus, whose greed for it allows him to say callously of his disinherited brother's fiancée, Florence: 'It seems the proper thing that she shall pass with the rest of the family property to the true heir' (79). Her mother takes a similar view: 'Why should not Florence be transferred with the remainder of the property?' (36). Florence, in the familiar Trollopian role of unshakable female fidelity, rejects such exploitative calculation: 'This was intolerable to Florence, – this idea that she should have been considered as capable of being intended for the purposes of other people' (113).

Scarborough's profound complaisance and wry delight in triumphing over legal machinery, the law of entail, and conventional respectability occasion some sharp comic irony, when, inspired by terrible malice against his mean-spirited son Augustus, he turns to affecting pious esteem for legal niceties. The law of entail requires that the estate – that is, 'things real, . . . such as are permanent, fixed, and immoveable' – go to the eldest legitimate son; but Scarborough also possesses considerable 'things personal . . . goods, money, and all other moveables',[15] which he determines to divert by means of his will to Mountjoy. Glowing with revengeful zeal, and aided by his medical attendant, Merton, he accordingly dictates a letter of instruction to Mr Grey. As well as the note of unction, notice both the artistry with which he contemplates the aesthetics of revenge and his special attention to the estate's timber:

> 'It is my purpose to make another will, and to leave everything that I am capable of leaving to my son Mountjoy. . . . I know the strength of an entail, and not for worlds would I venture to meddle with anything so holy.' There came a grin of satisfaction over his face as he uttered these words, and his scribe was utterly unable to keep from laughing. 'But as Augustus must have the acres, let him have them bare.'
> 'Underscore that word, if you please;' and the word was underscored. 'If I had time I would have every tree about the place cut down.'
> 'I don't think you could under the entail,' said Merton.
> 'I would use up every stick in building the farmers' barns and mending the farmers' gates, and I would cover an acre just in front of the house with a huge conservatory. I respect the law, my boy, and they would find it difficult to prove that I had gone beyond it. But there is not time for that kind of finished revenge.'   (369)

When, totally fed up with Augustus, Scarborough decides to disinherit him lock, stock and barrel and reinstate Mountjoy, Scarborough, with a look that combines 'the gleam of victory, and the glory of triumph, and the venom of malice', piously explains his action to Augustus as 'Just the ordinary way in which things ought to be allowed to run. Mr Grey, who is a very good man, persuaded me. No man ought to interfere with the law' (543). Scarborough's irony here is all the sharper in that Augustus, who is a barrister, has expressed himself deeply satisfied with his brother's loss on the grounds that 'The making of all right and wrong in this world depends on the law' (45). 'Augustus liked the law, – unless when in particular points it interfered with his own actions' (188).

The degree of Scarborough's growing enmity towards Augustus is seen in that reference to destroying the estate's timber. An estate's trees are generally regarded with special reverence, an index of the tenant's moral character and social responsibility, as they are in Jane Austen.[16] Legally, Scarborough can entertain such a shocking idea because he is a tenant in fee-tail, since 'A tenant in fee-tail has the same uncontrolled and unlimited power in committing waste, as a tenant in fee-simple.'[17] ('Waste' here means reducing an estate to bad condition by damage or neglect.) Though a tenant with an interest only for life or a number of years would be liable to recovery of 'the thing or place wasted, and also treble damages by the statute of Glocester [6 Edw. I. c. 5],'[18] a tenant in fee-tail can do as he likes. In Thackeray's *Barry Lyndon*, for example, when Barry 'determined to endow [his own] darling boy, Bryan, with a property, and to this end cut down twelve thousand pounds' worth of timber on Lady Lyndon's Yorkshire and Irish estates,' the guardian of young Bullingdon, the proper heir, was quite right to protest that Barry 'had no right to touch a stick of the trees,' since Barry 'had only a life-interest upon the Lyndon property.'[19] For, says Blackstone, 'Odious in the sight of the law is waste and destruction,' and 'if the particular tenant, I say, commits or suffers any waste, it is a manifest injury to him that has the inheritance, as it tends to mangle and dismember it of its most desirable incidents and ornaments, among which timber and houses may justly be reckoned the principal.'[20] Even 'a tenant for life without impeachment of waste' – that is, one who by his lease may commit waste for his own benefit without being sued – must nevertheless refrain from 'making *spoil and destruction* upon the estate.'[21] Such malicious destruction beyond what the tenant may reasonably do for his own profit is called, in somewhat humorous legal language, 'equitable waste', so called because actionable in a court of equity under the Lord Chancellor.[22] Scarborough, in fact, has a counterpart, at least in motive, in the defendant whose case established the difference between allowable waste and malicious, or equitable waste:

> This distinction was first introduced in the case of Lord Barnard, who was tenant for life without impeachment of waste, with remainder to his eldest son in tail; and having conceived a displeasure against his son, from motives of spleen, began to pull down the family mansion, Raby Castle; but he was restrained by the chancellor, and ordered to repair it. 2 *Vern.* 738. Since that case, such a tenant has been restrained from cutting down avenues and ornamental timber in pleasure grounds, and also young trees not fit for timber; and also trees upon a common two miles distant from the mansion house, which had been planted as an ornament to the estate. I *Bro.* 166. 3 *Bro.* 549. 6 *Ves. jun.* 107.[23]

As a tenant in fee-tail, that need not bother Scarborough unduly; nevertheless, should any objection arise, Scarborough has an instinct for the sort of argument that might weigh in his favour with the Lord Chancellor. Using the wood for 'building the farmer's barns and mending the farmer's gates' would have an air of demonstrating not malicious spoil and destruction but solicitude in the upkeep of the estate. And covering 'an acre just in front of the house with a huge conservatory' could be seen in the light of concern for improvement, though Scarborough's real intent, of course, comes as close to a scorched-earth policy as the law could be hoodwinked into allowing. 'I wonder,' he says, in a fit of malign reverie, 'whether I could scrape the paper off the drawing-room walls, and leave the scraps to his brother, without interfering with the entail' (371). Mr Grey, of course, is the fly in his ointment. Scarborough instructs his trustees, Mr Grey and Mr Bullfist, to sell 'everything which it would be in the squire's legal power to bequeath. The books, the gems, the furniture, both at Tretton and in London, the plate, the stock, the farm-produce, the pictures on the walls, and the wine in the cellars' (386). When, however, he broaches the sale of the timber, 'to this Mr Grey would not assent. "There would be an air of persecution about it," he said, "and it mustn't be done."' Nevertheless, since even Mr Grey has had his fill of Augustus by this time, 'to the general stripping of Tretton for the benefit of Mountjoy he gave a cordial agreement' (386).

The beneficiary of this legal thunderbolt shows a touching reaction to it. The most valuable part of what he is to inherit is the library of ten thousand volumes, which the hulking Guards-captain strolls in to inspect on an afternoon when it is too late to shoot birds and the hounds are not nearby. 'He took out book after book, and told himself with something of sadness in his heart that they were all "caviare" to him' (510). One contains an insuperable sentence of sixteen lines, and Wither's *Hallelujah* floors him. Mentally pricing the whole library, he gloomily reflects that 'three or four days at the club might see an end of it all' (511). His state of mind is complex: contrite over his gambling, appreciative of his father's attempts to assist him, understanding of Scarborough's compulsion to preserve the estate, but still ready to sue about his alleged illegitimacy, only partly because of his brother's greedy coldness, mostly because of the aspersion cast on his mother's memory. Property, legality, self-interest do not weigh with him heavily; filial sentiment for his mother does.

Mr Grey, who warms to Mountjoy even to lending him money, is one of Trollope's most attractive lawyers, an attorney with 'a well-earned reputation for professional acuteness and honesty' (172), not obtuse about his own feelings like Furnival of *Orley Farm*, not pompously condescending like Sir Abraham Haphazard of *The Warden*, not remotely as untroubled as Chaffanbrass. Mr Grey is the perfect, if rather tragic, foil for Scarborough, not only in honouring the law, but in his confidence about the stability of facts. (Here is Trollope sharing the Victorian epistemological anxiety again.) Grey is sure he cannot be tricked twice: 'Such facts, when made certain, are immovable,' he declares (518). But when Scarborough announces a second set of facts about his marriage, reinstating Mountjoy, though Grey

> persisted in not believing the story which had been told to him, he did in truth believe it. He believed at any rate in Mr. Scarborough. Mr. Scarborough had determined that the

property should go hither and thither according to his will,
without reference to the established laws of the land, and
had carried and would carry his purpose. . . . Mr.
Scarborough had turned him round his finger this way and
that way, just as he had pleased.   (525–6)

Their professional bond of lawyer and client is swallowed up
eventually in a mysterious human attachment wherein
exasperation vies with love. Scarborough assesses Grey's
apparent honesty as a mask adopted for success in business,
and Grey is repeatedly outraged by Scarborough's scandalous
frivolity about the law, yet Grey 'did not regard him as an
honest man regards a rascal, and was angry with himself in
consequence. He knew that there remained with him even
some spark of love for Mr. Scarborough which to himself was
inexplicable' (373). So with Scarborough: 'Thinking Mr. Grey
to be in some respects idiotic, he respected him, and almost
loved him. He thoroughly believed Mr. Grey, thinking him to
be an ass for telling so much truth unnecessarily' (195).
(Twain's dictum, 'Truth is the most valuable thing we have.
Let us economize it,' would have appealed to Scarborough.)
So when Grey lends money to the compulsive gambler,
Mountjoy, Scarborough writes: 'You are the most foolish man
I know with your money. To have given it to such a scapegrace
as my son Mountjoy! But you are the sweetest and finest
gentleman I ever came across' (478). Grey wishes to believe
that justice and the law coincide; Scarborough holds such an
equation ludicrous; but both value a notion of decency that is
the more moving for resisting easy formulation.[24]
    Mr Grey leaves the novel rather sadly, outwitted at every
turn by his own client. His partner, Mr Barry, who ten years
since considered Mr Grey both truthful and wise, now seems
'to think, in discussing the matter with the favourite clerk, that
the older the bird became the more often he could be caught
with chaff' (558). Mr Barry takes the view that Scarborough
'has been so clever that he ought to be forgiven all his rascality'
(563), indeed that he is 'the best lawyer he ever knew' (599).
For his part, Mr Grey notices that his partner himself is
'tending towards sharp practice' and 'beginning to love his
clients, – not with a proper attorney's affection, as his children, but as sheep to be shorn. . . . Mr. Grey, as he thought of

these things, began to fancy that his own style of business was becoming antiquated. . . . he would put his house in order, and leave the firm' (559). Mr Grey is made to feel old and *passé* not just by his younger partner but by old Scarborough himself: 'Though I call him old, he was ever so much younger than I am' (599). Grey, of course, is right in a sense; he is the voice of the super-ego – honest, truthful, respectable, mature – confronted with an embodiment of the id, cunning, amoral, impudent, immensely self-satisfied, child-like in zest even on the brink of the grave.

One might choose other than psychiatric abstractions to compare Grey and Scarborough; as Bradford Booth observes, 'nowhere else in Trollope's work is a complete novel so susceptible of an allegorical interpretation.'[25] Trollope even nudges us with Dolly Grey's allegory. She calls Mr Barry 'the Devil'. 'Her father she had dubbed "Reason", and herself "Conscience"' (312). Dolly functions as conscience in delicious midnight conversations in her father's bedroom about the moral intricacies of his various cases:

> the eloquent barrister, or it might be the client himself, startled sometimes at the amount of enthusiasm which Mr. Grey would throw into his argument, would little dream that the very words had come from the young lady in her dressing-gown. . . . Miss Grey thoroughly liked these discussions. . . . They formed, indeed, the very salt of her life. (152)

Reactions to Dolly's relationship with her father, 'the only man for whom she had ever felt the slightest regard' (148), and the only man she would have for a husband if she could choose, vary. In their isolation, advocating 'old ways . . . now so bizarre that she appears freakish,' and in their personal relationship, James Kincaid sees the sombre effect of a society with disintegrating values: 'Trollope's most open excursion into twisted sexuality marks an appropriate symbol', he says, 'for a world that so distorts all the values which count.'[26] One might add that the tension between world and conscience, Caesar and God, though locatable in Victorian society, is a perennial one. And the father–daughter relationship, though 'twisted' in an obvious sense, is also, after the tense bond between Grey and Scarborough, the most touching and intricate in the book, infinitely more interesting than the untwisted relationship between Harry Annesley, 'the hero of this story', and his resolute Florence. Still, at the level of impression, how much of the novel's peculiar force comes of its recurrent and intense focus in two bedrooms. In one, old Scarborough, with the awesome imperativeness of his imminent death, rules his world like a spider in the middle of his web, his filaments spread about the country. People come to *him*, and attend his pleasure. In the other, enclosed by the night, a fretting Grey picks over the crises of conscience occasioned by Scarborough's will, the reclusive company of his daughter accentuating the loneliness of moral tribulation and the eccentricity of such scruple in the striving world around them.

In a fine example of Trollope's structural skill, the law of entail that provides an armature for the main plot also holds together the lighter-toned subplot in which Harry Annesley is 'the acknowledged heir to his mother's brother' (22). Squire Prosper, whose estate, Buston, Harry is to inherit, educates Harry at Charterhouse and Cambridge and, on the assumption that an heir need not fit himself for a profession, provides him with £250 a year. But Harry does not behave as his uncle would like, showing a flippant distaste for his uncle's vanity in mumbling family sermons and, moreover, becoming involved in a scandal by fighting Mountjoy Scarborough over the woman they both love. When Prosper huffily considers means to break his connection with his insubordinate heir, Harry is discomfited.

> He had been told that he was the heir, not to the uncle, but to Buston, and had gradually been taught to look upon Buston as his right, – as though he had a certain indefeasible property in the acres. He now began to perceive that there was no such thing. A tacit contract had been made on his behalf [the sermons], and he had declined to accept his share of the contract. (233–4)

The legal situation here is clear enough. Since Prosper is without issue, Harry will inherit Buston as the son of Prosper's nearest kin, his sister. Though Prosper lacks Scarborough's diabolical ingenuity at defeating the laws of inheritance, he has two options. First, though a reclusive and 'sickly little man about fifty' (22), he can bestir himself to marry and beget an heir. (Trollope knew this situation well from family experience: listing his father's woes in *An Autobiography*, he concludes, 'Then, as a final crushing blow, an old uncle, whose heir he was to have been, married and had a family!' [3][27]) Casting a connubial eye over the district, Prosper singles out Miss Matilda Thoroughbung, who, though the daughter of a family of brewers, possesses £25 000 and is forty-two, still of child-bearing age. The second thing Prosper can do to frustrate Harry's hopes, even if the anticipated heir is not begotten, is, as Harry's mother anxiously observes, to 'settle a jointure on [Matilda] which would leave the property not worth having' (214). A jointure, as Sir Edward Coke defines it, is 'a competent livelihood of freehold for the wife, of lands and tenements . . . for the life of the wife at least'.[28]

Although the attempted disinheritance of Harry provides a symmetrical reflection of the main plot, the chief interest of Mr Prosper's legal problems arises from the complicated emotional tangle he gets into over this matter of the jointure. Profoundly smug about his status as a gentleman – 'Miss Thoroughbung was hardly a lady' (247) – Prosper in his proposal to her is ready to linger on the rhetoric of sentiment, if he could only remember it, and leave the sordid details of property to the arrangement of mere lawyers. But to his very uncomfortable surprise Miss Thoroughbung has no such seemly reticence:

> 'The lawyers are very well; but in a transaction of this kind there is nothing like the principals understanding each other. Young women are always robbed when their money is left altogether to the gentlemen.'
> 'Robbed!'
> 'Don't suppose I mean you, Mr. Prosper; and the robbery I mean is not considered disgraceful at all. The gentlemen I mean are the fathers and the brothers, and the uncles and the lawyers. And they intend to do right after the custom of their fathers and uncles. But woman's rights are coming up.'
> 'I hate woman's rights.'

'Nevertheless they are coming up. A young woman doesn't get taken in as she used to do. . . . Since woman's rights have come up a young woman is better able to fight her own battle.'

Mr. Prosper was willing to admit that Miss Thoroughbung was fair, but she was fat also, and at least forty. There was hardly need that she should refer so often to her own unprotected youth.   (249)

Poor Squire Prosper – barely into his proposal and already appalled by his prospective spouse! Neither touched by his sentiment nor subdued by his masculine magnanimity, she lists her conditions in professional detail, itemising the disposal of her income, the inheritances of possible offspring, her household expenses including champagne, and her need for a carriage and ponies (the ponies might seem a minor affair, but much will ride on them). Her cognisance that, if a daughter instead of a son is born, the daughter will not inherit, indicates further intentions to protect the daughter. This brisk specifying of terms is all too much for Prosper, but as he drives home he fears that 'a strong foundation had been laid for a breach of promise case if he were to attempt to escape' (251).

The legal situation is what holds this bundle of conflicting interests and passions together in all its intricacy. Harry as potential heir can be simply set aside if Prosper begets that son. And the jointure his mother fears as leaving the property 'not worth having' can also deprive him of full enjoyment of the estate. Tenancy in dower gave wives a third of an entailed estate for life, but, says Blackstone, 'upon preconcerted marriages, and in estates of considerable consequence, tenancy in dower happens very seldom'[29] – the stakes being high, complications possible, and bargains to be struck, people preferred jointures instead; that is, a settlement in lieu of dower. In *Ralph the Heir* Trollope gives some idea of the bargaining involved. Ralph is 'to give everything and to get nothing'. Why the girl's father 'should have demanded out of such a property as that of Newton a jointure of £4000 a year, with a house to be found either in town or country, as the widow might desire, on behalf of a penniless girl, no one acting in the Newton interest could understand' (II, 334).

After some sharp words Carey, Ralph's lawyer, arranges quickly that 'the dower must be £2000, out of which the widow must find her own house' (II, 335). Under the circumstances, then, Miss Thoroughbung's conditions – remember, she has £25 000 and an annual income of £972 6s. 8d. – might seem to a modern eye realistic, even modest. Her lawyers, Messrs Soames and Simpson, state them simply for Prosper:

> They had proposed to her that the use of her own income should be by deed left to herself. Some proportion of it should go into the house, and might be made matter of agreement. They suggested that an annuity of a thousand pounds a year, in shape of dower, should be secured to their client in the event of her outliving Mr. Prosper. The estate, should, of course, be settled on the eldest child. The mother's property should be equally divided among the other children. Buston Hall should be the residence of the widow till the eldest son should be twenty-four, after which Mr. Prosper would no doubt feel that their client would have to provide a home for herself.   (258)

Prosper, who sought marriage more in spite than ardour, and who is appalled by a woman with sense, a woman who talks of rights, is not to be pleased. 'The letter made Mr. Prosper very angry' (258). He needs a straw to clutch at, and he finds it in those ponies Miss Thoroughbung craves. They suggest a style repugnant to his reclusive nature. The greater his loathing for his prospective bride, the more 'the ponies grew in imagination, and became enormous horses capable of consuming any amount of oats. Mr. Prosper was not of a stingy nature, but he had already perceived that his escape, if it were effected, must be made good by means of those ponies' (420). Accordingly, as negotiations continue, a pony becomes 'an animal which of its very nature was objectionable to him. There was a want of dignity in a pony to which Buston Hall should never be subjected' (462).

From the beginning Prosper saw 'a lack of dignity about Miss Thoroughbung herself' (462), a lack reflected in her lawyers' status, another element in the legal interest of the novel. 'Messrs. Grey and Barry, of Lincoln's Inn, were his lawyers, who were quite gentlemen. He knew nothing against

Messrs. Soames and Simpson, but he thought that their work consisted generally in the recovery of local debts' (258); thus the letter about Miss Thoroughbung's terms, 'coming to him through these local lawyers, . . . was doubly distasteful' (259). They are lawyers, they are Miss Thoroughbung's lawyers, they are crass local lawyers. Triply distasteful!

Mr Grey, whom Prosper is pleased to think of as a gentleman, regards him as 'almost the biggest fool I have ever known' but also as 'a gentleman [who] . . . wants nothing but what is or ought to be his own' (259–60); so Grey decides to cut down the proposals of Soames and Simpson drastically. 'I have', says Grey, 'to make allowance for his folly, – a sort of windage which is not dishonest' (260). Grey would allow half Miss Thoroughbung's income to herself, the other half to her husband, a jointure of £250 in addition to the income from her property, and the settlement among the children as she proposes. As Miss Thoroughbung said, and evidently with reason, the gentlemen, 'the fathers and the brothers, and the uncles and the lawyers . . . intend to do right after the custom of their fathers and uncles' (249).

Earlier in the novel we are told that 'Mr. Prosper enjoyed greatly two things: the mysticism of being invisible, and the opportunity of writing a letter' (237). With legal mantraps set all about him by Soames and Simpson, both delights are soured. He must write to call off the marriage, but 'he was afraid that he might commit himself by an epithet. He dreaded even an adverb too much. He found that a full stop expressed his feelings too violently, and wrote the letter again, for the fifth time, because of the big initial which followed the full stop' (479). The consequence of all this close deliberation is that Miss Thoroughbung gets wind of the news through family rumour, beards him in his den, and picking up the letter offers an acerbic, sentence-by-sentence, on-the-spot practical criticism, concluding with a few caustic reflections on gentlemen:

> 'Oh yes; of course I shall keep it, and shall give it to Messrs Soames and Simpson. They are most gentlemanlike men, and will be shocked at such conduct as this from the squire of Buston. The letter will be published in the newspapers, of course. It will be very painful to me, no doubt; but I shall owe it to my sex to punish you. . . .'

She must have been aware that every word she spoke was a dagger. . . . Nothing could have wounded him more than the comparison between himself and Soames and Simpson. They were gentlemen! 'The vulgarest men in all Buntingford!' he declared to himself, and always ready for any sharp practice. Whereas he was no man . . .; a mean creature, altogether unworthy to be regarded as a gentleman. He knew himself to be Mr. Prosper of Buston Hall, with centuries of Prospers for his ancestors; whereas Soames was the son of a tax-gatherer; and Simpson had come down from London, as a clerk from a solicitor's office in the City. And yet it was true that people would talk of him as did Miss Thoroughbung!   (483–4)

Miss Thoroughbung, of course, is full of mirth. She suggests that the gentlemanly Soames and Simpson might consider £10 000 not too much salve to apply to her wounded feelings, and pronouncing, 'There's your letter, which, however, would be of no use because it is not signed. A very stupid letter it is' (486), she leaves him, paralysed with mortification, and content to come to terms with Harry.

Lawyers and the law enable Trollope to pursue most effectively his interest in the tensions between public behaviour and private scruple. As a context in which to elaborate such tensions, the law, like politics and the church, provides a hierarchical structure, one that descends from justice as a metaphysical principle, to the body of the law, to the representatives, interpreters and manipulators of the legal system – an ample field for adjustment, manoeuvre and accommodation.[30] *Mr Scarborough's Family* is a concentrated example of Trollope's recurrent legal curiosity, covering the ground from the relationship between natural and positive law down to the intricacies of entail and inheritance, the rights of waste, the bargaining of marriage contracts, and the personalities and social status of lawyers (and I have left out of account detective Prodgers' interest in Harry as the object of a criminal investigation involving the possible murder of Mountjoy). Not just because of its legal interest, but not apart from it either, this posthumous novel is a masterpiece somewhat lost in the sea of Trollope's plenty. Its intricate but crisp examination of moral ambiguities in social and personal behaviour, its ingenuity, its intriguing central character, its finely structured and integrated plot, its lean, ironic intelligence, kept up to the mark by Scarborough's wry acerbity, make it a brilliant achievement. Trollope is a novelist of fine moral distinctions, and the machinery of the law in this excellent novel gives him a convenient framework for articulating them, for creating 'the needed biting interest' – an appropriate phrase for describing the sardonic comedy of *Mr. Scarborough's Family*.

Notes and References

1 TROLLOPE AND THE LAW: A PROSPECT

1. Michael Sadleir, *Trollope: A Commentary* (London: Constable, 1927; revised 1945) pp. 52–3.
2. Coral Lansbury, *The Reasonable Man: Trollope's Legal Fiction* (Princeton: Princeton University Press, 1981) p. 13.
3. Ibid., p. 21.
4. Ibid.
5. Witt, *Life in the Law* (London: Laurie, 1906) p. 44.
6. Maria Edgeworth, *Castle Rackrent*, ed. George Watson, (Oxford: Oxford University Press World's Classics paperback, 1980) pp. 108–11. To equip himself for his Irish novels, Trollope read novels and tales of Irish life, including Maria Edgeworth and William Carleton (see Sadleir, pp. 143–4).
7. 'Mr. Trollope and the Lawyers', *London Review*, 8 Nov. 1862, p. 405.
8. See John Halperin, 'Trollope's *Phineas Finn* and History', *English Studies*, 59 (April 1978) pp. 121–3.
9. Jonathan Swift, *Gulliver's Travels*, Part IV, ch. v.
10. Thomas Macaulay, 'Francis Bacon' (1837), in *Critical and Historical Essays*, 2 vols (London: Dent Everyman edition, 1907), vol. II, p. 317.
11. James Boswell, *The Journal of a Tour to the Hebrides*, G. B. Hill and L. F. Powell (eds) (Oxford: Clarendon Press, 1950) 15 August 1773, pp. 26–7.
12. 'From the moment that any advocate can be permitted to say, that he *will* or will *not* stand between the crown and the subject arraigned in the court where he daily sits to practise, from that moment the liberties of England are at an end. If the advocate refuses to defend, from what *he may think* of the charge, or of the defence, he assumes the character of the judge; nay, he assumes it before the hour of judgement; and, in proportion to his rank and reputation, puts the heavy influence of perhaps a mistaken opinion into the scale against the accused, in whose favour the benevolent principle of English law makes all presumptions, and which commands the very judge to be his counsel.' *R. v. Paine* (1792), *State Trials*, vol. XXII, 357 at 412.
13. *Cornhill Magazine*, 3 (April, 1861) p. 447.
14. Ibid., pp. 456–7.
15. Ibid., pp. 458–9.
16. William Blackstone, *Commentaries on the Laws of England*, 4 vols (Oxford: 1745–9), vol. II, p. 116.

17. For an authoritative account of how entails were barred by common recoveries and fines, see R. Megarry and Wade, *The Law of Real Property*, 3rd edn (London: Stevens, 1966) pp. 87–9. 'These', they say, 'were products of legal ingenuity, contrived and perfected in a period notable for formalism and fictitious processes.' In essence, in a common recovery, the tenant conspired with a friend or buyer who laid claim to the land of the tenant (in accordance with their collusion, the friend had covertly bought it or agreed to reconvey it in fee simple to the tenant). But what about the prospective heirs? Well, a fictitious character was named who had warranted the tenant's title on penalty of providing lands of equal value if it were unsound. The court was not inconveniently curious about the identity of this warrantor. In common practice, the court crier acted the part for a small fee. The friend or buyer then took the matter up with the warrantor. They asked the court for a recess to talk it over, whereupon the warrantor would default by failing to reappear. The court would render judgement against this fictitious rascal, who was considered in contempt of court, confirm the friend's title, and the entail would go into limbo, or perhaps, considering Blackstone's language on the legal beauty of this abstract nonsense, into a state of divine translation: 'it hath been said', says Blackstone,

> that, though the estate-tail is gone from the recoveree, yet it is not *destroyed*, but only *transferred*; and still subsists, and will ever continue to subsist (by construction of law) in the recoverer, his heirs, and assigns: and, as the estate-tail so continues to subsist for ever, the remainders or reversions expectant on the determination of such estate-tail can never take place (*Commentaries*, II, p. 360).

One thinks:

> And little town, thy streets for evermore
> Will silent be; and not a soul to tell
> Why thou art desolate, can e'er return.

Bentham, naturally, despised all this: 'fiction', he says, 'is a *wart* which here and there deforms the face of justice: in English law, *fiction* is a *syphilis*, which runs in every vein and carries into every part of the system the principle of rottenness'. (*The Art of Packing Special Juries* [1821], in *The Works of Jeremy Bentham*, ed. John Bowring, 11 vols [1838–43; reprinted New York: Russell and Russell, 1962] vol. V, p. 28). The Fines and Recoveries Act of 1833 put an end to fines and recoveries and substituted a straightforward way of barring entails.

18. R. Megarry and H. W. R. Wade, *The Law of Real Property*, p. 289. See also Sir Frederick Pollock, *The Land Laws*, 3rd edn (London: Macmillan, 1896) pp. 111–14.

19. First Report, Parliamentary Papers 1829, vol. X, pp. 6–7; and Sir William Holdsworth, *A History of English Law*, 17 vols (London: Methuen & Sweet and Maxwell, 1903–66) vol. XV, p. 169.

20. Walter Bagehot, *The English Constitution*, (London: Oxford University Press World's Classics edition, 1928) p. 145.

21. A. V. Dicey, 'The Paradox of the Land Law', *Law Quarterly Review*, (1905) pp. 221–2.
22. See Richard D. Altick, *Victorian Studies in Scarlet* (New York: Norton, 1970).
23. This critical zeal has not died out. Popular capacity for considering the fine points of crime, legal procedure, and the actors in the legal drama, was demonstrated to me afresh when, to get the feel of the place for the writing of this book, I visited the Old Bailey. The trial was for murder. And my fellow spectators, as I found when the judge, after some caustic remarks to a badly prepared counsel, called a recess to let him repair his shortcomings, consisted, as it seemed, of a number of old lags, habitués of the Old Bailey, who fell to matching notes on the judge, the counsel, and the defendants (with whom they seemed to be on neighbourly terms) with a nicety of comparison, discrimination and accumulated knowledge that would have done credit to any scholarly enterprise.
24. See Philip Collins, ch. IX, 'The Police', in *Dickens and Crime* (London: Macmillan, 1962).
25. See Keith Hollingsworth, *The Newgate Novel, 1830–1847* (Detroit: Wayne State University Press, 1963).
26. See Michael Timko, 'The Victorianism of Victorian Literature', *New Literary History*, 6 (1975) pp. 607–27.
27. See my chapter, 'The Curse of Words in *He Knew He Was Right*', in Juliet and Rowland McMaster, *The Novel from Sterne to James* (London: Macmillan, 1981) pp. 195–212.
28. Possibly Trollope had read another of James Fitzjames Stephen's deflating articles on popular novelists, 'Detectives in Fiction and in Real Life', in *Saturday Review*, no. 17 (11 June 1864) pp. 712–13, where Stephen scornfully remarks:

> That an *atra cura*, or rather a *caerulea* or dark-blue *cura*, sits behind every criminal, and hunts him down in a second-class railway carriage with the sagacity of a Red Indian, the scent of a bloodhound, and an unlimited command of all the resources of modern science, appears to be a cherished belief with a certain class of novelists. . . The whole matter may be summed up very shortly. There is little scope for ingenuity in the detection of crimes, because, if there is evidence, it is almost always easy to produce it; and if there is none, it is altogether impossible to get it. The sphere of ingenuity is in making guesses, and the whole object of English courts of law and rules of evidence is to exclude guesswork.

29. In *The Three Clerks* Trollope as narrator admits, of the Old Bailey, 'I have never seen the place' (p. 475) and excuses himself from giving a circumstantial amount of a trial by saying he would only be copying 'the proceedings at some of those modern *causes célèbres* with which all who love such matters are familiar' (p. 483).
30. See Henry S. Drinker, 'The Lawyers of Anthony Trollope', in *Two Addresses Delivered to Members of the Grolier Club* (New York: Grolier Club, 1950).
31. Trollope, To ?, 4 April 1879, in *The Letters of Anthony Trollope*, ed. John

Hall, 2 vols (Stanford: Stanford University Press, 1983) vol. II, p. 821.

32. See particularly John Halperin, 'Trollope and Feminism', *The South Atlantic Quarterly*, 77 (1978) pp. 179–88; Juliet McMaster, 'The Men and Women', in *Trollope's Palliser Novels: Theme and Pattern* (London: Macmillan, 1978) pp. 155–79; Ruth apRoberts, 'Emily and Nora and Dorothy and Priscilla and Jemima and Cary', in *The Victorian Experience: The Novelists*, ed. Richard A. Levine (Athens Ohio: Ohio University Press, 1976) pp. 87–120; and R. D. McMaster, 'Women in *The Way We Live Now*', *English Studies in Canada*, 7 (1981), pp. 66–80.

33. Tennyson, *The Princess* (1847); Ruskin, 'Of Queens' Gardens', in *Sesame and Lilies* (1865); Huxley, 'Emancipation – Black and White', in *The Reader* (1865), reprinted in *Science and Education, Essays* (1893); Taylor, 'Enfranchisement of Women', *Westminster and Foreign Review* (1851); John Stuart Mill, *On the Subjection of Women* (1869).

34. An excellent and concise discussion of the subject is Lee Holcombe's 'Victorian Wives and Property: Reform of the Married Women's Property Law, 1857–1882', in *A Widening Sphere: Changing Roles of Victorian Women*, ed. Martha Vicinus (Bloomington: Indiana University press, 1980) pp. 3–28.

35. J. S. McMaster, *Trollope's Palliser Novels: Theme and Pattern*, p. 177.

36. Edward Lytton Bulwer discusses the political and class significances of the marriage market in *England and the English* (1833).

37. Holcombe, p. 12.

2 SEX IN THE BARRISTER'S CHAMBERS: LAWYER AND CLIENT IN *ORLEY FARM*

1. Contemporary reviews were generally hostile to Trollope's handling of law in *Orley Farm*. The most knowledgeable was 'Mr. Trollope and the Lawyers', *London Review*, 8 Nov. 1862, pp. 405–7. Others were in *The Times*, 26 Dec. 1862, p. 5; *The Saturday Review*, 11 Oct. 1862, pp. 444–5; *The National Review*, Jan. 1863, pp. 27–40; *The Home and Foreign Review*, Jan. 1863, pp. 291–4. Modern accounts by lawyers include a witty attack by Sir Francis Newbolt, 'Regina versus Mason', *Nineteenth Century*, 95 (1924) pp. 227–36 and a more sympathetic study by H. S. Drinker, 'The Lawyers of Trollope', in *Two Addresses Delivered to Members of the Grolier Club* (New York: The Grolier Club, 1949). A. O. J. Cockshutt in *Anthony Trollope* (London: Collins, 1955) p. 166, says 'Trollope's knowledge of the law was sketchy'. James Kincaid in *The Novels of Anthony Trollope* (Oxford: Clarendon Press, 1977) p. 80, sees a tension between theory and practice, both inadequate to stay the disintegration of communal values: 'principles become quixotic abstractions, practice mere vicious opportunism, the attempt to deny truth'. P. D. Edwards, closer to the tenor of my chapter in some respects, sees Trollope's attack on the legal system as 'little more than a smoke-screen of moral indignation, behind which he works his novel to an end that he fears the fastidious reader may think morally subversive', in

Anthony Trollope: His Art and Scope (Hassocks: Harvester Press, 1978) p. 90. The most comprehensive treatment, taking in the major themes and characters, is in Coral Lansbury's *The Reasonable Man: Trollope's Legal Fictions* (Princeton: Princeton University Press, 1981).

2. Robert M. Polhemus, *The Changing World of Anthony Trollope*, p. 85. (Berkeley and Los Angeles: University of California Press, 1968) p. 68.

3. *The London Review*, 8 Nov. 1862, p. 407.

4. Trollope uses the terms 'attorney' and 'solicitor' interchangeably. Samuel Warren, in *Moral, Social and Professional Duties of Attorneys and Solicitors*, 1848, notes that the term 'solicitor' is a 'modern new-fangled one, which would erroneously lead people to think such persons have no rights to practise in the Courts of Law, but are confined to Courts of Chancery' because the proper alternatives were 'Attorney at Law' and 'Solicitor in Equity' (p. 347). Warren vigorously prefers 'attorney', but 'solicitor' was becoming the more fashionable term.

5. Harry Kirk, in *Portrait of a Profession: A History of the Solicitor's Profession, 1100 to the Present Day* (London: Oyez Publishing, 1976) pp. 172–4, discusses the establishment and questioning of this etiquette learnedly. See also Brian Abel-Smith and Robert Stevens, *Lawyers and the Courts: A Sociological Study of the English Legal System* (Cambridge, Mass.: Harvard, 1967) pp. 21 and 57; Michael Birks, *Gentlemen of the Law* (London: Stevens, 1960) p. 196; and Sir William Holdsworth, *History of English Law*, 17 vols (London: Methuen, 1903–66) vol. VI, 444; vol. XII, 74; and vol. XV, 427.

6. Minutes, 27 June 1800, quoted by Kirk, *Portrait of a Profession*, p. 172.

7. *Bennet* v. *Hale* (1850) 15 Q.B. 171.

8. Kirk, *Portrait of a Profession*, p. 173.

9. Ibid., p. 174.

10. Snubbin is ill-washed and slovenly, like Chaffanbrass. He smiles at Pickwick's errand – which is to tell him 'that I am innocent of the falsehood laid to my charge' – then stops listening and changes the subject. *Pickwick Papers* (London: Oxford University Press, New Oxford Illustrated Edition, 1948) pp. 427–31.

11. *Bennet* v. *Hale* (1850) 15 Q.B. 180.

12. R. E. Megarry, *Lawyer and Litigant in England* (London: Stevens, 1962) p. 14.

13. See Ruth apRoberts, *Trollope: Artist and Moralist* (London: Chatto and Windus, 1971) p. 76.

14. Thackeray, *The Letters and Private Papers of William Makepeace Thackeray*, ed. Gordon N. Ray, 4 vols (London: Oxford University Press, 1946) vol. IV, p. 115.

15. Judges, 2:17.

16. I Kings, 11.

17. Samuel Warren, for example, addressing solicitors, says that despite popular opinions about the eagerness of lawyers for litigation, 'it is your duty, and ought ever to be your object, to *prevent* litigation' (*Moral, Social and Professional Duties of Attorneys and Solicitors*, 1848, p. 232).

18. Chaffanbrass too, however, takes note of the etiquette of conferences. Conferences with barristers occur in the barrister's chambers, and only

exceptionally in the solicitor's. Thus when Chaffanbrass is encountered in Aram's office, Trollope observes,

> It is not quite the thing for a barrister to wait upon an attorney, and therefore it must not be supposed that Mr. Chaffanbrass had come to Mr. Aram with any view to business; but, nevertheless, as the two men understood each other, they could say what they had to say as to this case of Lady Mason's, although their present positions were somewhat irregular. (II, p. 219)

19. See, for example, P. D. Edwards' discussion of responses to her by Trollope and his readers in *Anthony Trollope: His Art and Scope*, pp. 108–13.

20. In *Robert Browning*, ed. Isobel Armstrong, in the series 'Writers and their Backgrounds' (London: Bell, 1974) pp. 270–1.

21. Trollope makes one interesting legal comment apropos of Furnival during the interview: Furnival 'was strongly convinced of her guilt, but by no means strongly convinced that her guilt could be proved.' An un-Trollopian barrister might reflect that it is not the barrister's function to usurp the role of judge and jury but only to make the client's case. Furnival has an opinion. In the trial he expresses an opposite opinion. Either way, barristers have been reprimanded by judges for interjecting their personal convictions into the legal argument. In the famous 1856 trial of William Palmer, the poisoner, Serjeant Shee, for example, was taken to task by the Attorney-General, and reprimanded by Chief Justice Campbell, for expressing to the jury his conviction that Palmer was innocent.

22. Walter Kendrick writes:

> Trollope's characters, indeed, are about equally aware of both their conscious and their unconscious thoughts. In regard to both they possess a third faculty that listens, and that acts upon the advice given to it by either the conscious or the unconscious voice. Both voices are rhetorical, oratorical: the Trollopian mind is a sort of internal debating society, containing an audience and two speakers who compete for their listener's attention. The difference between the orators is principally one of value: the unconscious voice is always the right one, and those of Trollope's characters who achieve happiness do so because, after however long a period of vacillation, they allow the unconscious voice to tell them what to do (*The Novel-Machine: The Theory and Fiction of Anthony Trollope* [Baltimore and London: Johns Hopkins University Press, 1980] p. 87).

This assessment of a psychological awkwardness as a rhetorical technique does not seem to help here. It compounds the problem of the unconscious being conscious by adding 'awareness' of the unconscious to it. And the unconscious voice here could hardly be seen as 'right' in any other than a Spencerian sense of furthering advantage in sex or survival.

3 MR CHAFFANBRASS FOR THE DEFENCE:
   TROLLOPE AND THE OLD BAILEY TRADITION

1. 6 & 7 William IV c. 114. See also Sir William Holdsworth, *A History of English Law*, 17 vols (London: Methuen, 1903–66), XI, p. 555 and XV, p. 157.
2. J. H. Baker, *An Introduction to English Legal History* (London: Butterworth, 1979) p. 418.
3. Sir Henry Hawkins (Baron Brampton), *The Reminiscences of Sir Henry Hawkins*, ed. Richard Harris, KC (London: Nelson, 1904) p. 38.
4. William Ballantine, *Some Experiences of a Barristers's Life*, 2 vols (London: Bentley, 1882) vol. I, p. 80.
5. Bernard O'Donnell, *The Old Bailey and its Trials* (London: Clerke & Cockeran, 1950) pp. 158–60. See also Peter Archer, *The Queen's Courts* (Harmondsworth: Penguin Books, 1956) pp. 70–1.
6. Ballantine, *Some Experiences of a Barrister's Life*, vol. I, pp. 79 and 105.
7. O'Donnell, *The Old Bailey and its Trials*, p. 18.
8. Montagu Williams, QC, *Leaves of a Life: Being the Reminiscences of Montagu Williams, QC* (London: Macmillan, 1893) p. 162.
9. Theodore Hook, *Gilbert Gurney*, 3 vols (London: Whittaker, 1836) vol. II, p. 98.
10. Hawkins, *The Reminiscences of Sir Henry Hawkins*, p. 41.
11. Baker, *An Introduction to English Legal History*, p. 417.
12. Ballantine, *Some Experiences of a Barrister's Life*, vol. I, p. 80.
13. John George Witt, KC, *Life in the Law* (London: Laurie, 1906) p. 69.
14. Ibid., pp. 69–70. See also Henry Cecil, *Brief to Council* (London: Michael Joseph, 1958) pp. 47–8.
15. Hawkins, *The Reminiscences of Sir Henry Hawkins*, p. 38.
16. J. M. Langford, 7 March 1877, National Library of Scotland MS #4361, quoted in F. D. Tredrey, *The House of Blackwood 1804–1954: The History of a Publishing Firm* (Edinburgh: Blackwood, 1954) p. 261.
17. Ballantine, *Some Experiences of a Barrister's Life*, vol. I, 124.
18. Witt, *Life in the Law*, p. 49.
19. Hawkins, especially, in his *Reminiscences*, finds such judicial lapses amusing. In Chapter 3, Platt, a 'kind' counsel gets 'a very respectable but ignorant labouring man' to discuss odours as colours, then plies the thoroughly agonised witness with Latin quotations to the vast amusement of the court and judge, 'who could not keep his countenance'. An awesome example of callousness thought to be amusing is the conclusion of Chapter 12 on Graham, 'the polite judge'.
20. R. E. Megarry, *Lawyer and Litigant in England* (London: Stevens, 1962) p. 128.
21. Coral Lansbury, in *The Reasonable Man: Trollope's Legal Fiction* (Princeton: Princeton University Press, 1981) p. 36, probably following Henry S. Drinker in 'The Lawyers of Anthony Trollope', in *Two Addresses Delivered to Members of the Grolier Club* (New York: Grolier Club, 1950) p. 29, mistakes the defendant, the questions and Trollope's reaction, having him almost exploding with rage. In fact, he was impudently

amusing, as the report shows. I am grateful to the National Library of Ireland for supplying me with copies of the newspaper reports.

22. Mr Brereton's sorry and impertinent sally is presumably based on the Scandinavian word, troll, for supernatural beings, imps, witches.
23. Justin McCarthy, *Reminiscences*, 2 vols (New York: Harpers, 1899) vol. I, p. 372.
24. The reporter probably misheard the name. It should be O'Laugher.
25. The passage referred to is in Chapter 29:

> Had that piece of red moreen been gifted with an ear to hear, and a tongue to tell, what an indifferent account would it give of the veracity of judges and of the consciences of lawyers! How many offences had it heard stigmatised by his lordship as the most heinous that had ever been brought before him in his judicial capacity! How many murderers, felons, and robbers, described as poor harmless, innocent, foolish boys, brought into trouble by a love of frolic! How many witnesses, vainly endeavouring to tell the truth, forced by the ingenuity of lawyers into falsehood and perjury! What awful denunciations and what light wit, almost in the same breath! . . . (*The Macdermots of Ballycloran*, p. 532)

26. 'What is Justice?' asks Carlyle, 'The clothed embodied Justice that sits in Westminster Hall, with penalties, parchments, tipstaves, is very visible. But the *un*embodied Justice, whereof that other is either an emblem, or else is a fearful indescribability, is not so visible! For the unembodied Justice is of Heaven; a Spirit, and Divinity of Heaven, – *in*visible to all but the noble and the pure of soul. The impure ignoble gaze with eyes, and she is not there.' *Past and Present* (London: Dent Everyman edition, 1912) p. 13.
27. Megarry, *Lawyer and Litigant in England*, pp. 155–6.
28. Quoted and discussed by William Forsyth in *Hortensius: An Historical Essay on the Office and Duties of an Advocate*, 3rd edn (London: Murray, 1879) p. 389.
29. Holdsworth, *A History of English Law*, vol. XIII, p. 656, and vol. XV, p. 441.
30. When Forsyth quoted Brougham's famous remark in the first edition of *Hortensius* (1849), Brougham wrote the above explanation to him, and Forsyth included it in subsequent editions. As Holdsworth notes, however (*A History of English Law*, vol. XIII, p. 656), Brougham was holding to the remark unqualified in 1864. Forsyth discusses the ethics of advocacy at length and with interesting examples in Chapter X, 'Forensic Casuistry'.
31. The *London Review*, 8 November 1862, pp. 405–7. The reviewer also remarks that it is unjust to take Mr. Edwin James as representative of the Bar. In *Anthony Trollope: His Work, Associates and Literary Originals* (London: John Lane, 1913) p. 194, T. H. S. Escott, suggesting that Trollope drew Chaffanbrass from many originals, recalls Trollope saying of James: 'I had scarcely ever seen him, out of court or in it, but I have been told he had Chaffanbrass's habit of constantly arranging and re-arranging his wig, and of sometimes, for effect, dropping his voice so

low that it could scarcely be heard.' Investigated by his Inn in 1861, James was found to be guilty of various swindles including, when acting for a plaintiff, borrowing £1,250 from the defendant, saying he would let him off light in cross-examination. Disbarred in 1861, he went to America, practised at the New York Bar and went upon the stage. He published *Political Institutions of America and England* in 1872 and died in London, 1882.

32. Henry S. Drinker, in his 'The Lawyers of Anthony Trollope', divides Trollope's treatment of lawyers into three phases, a pre-London period to 1860, a transition in *Orley Farm* in which the lawyers become more human, and the London period after 1861 when Trollope 'met and associated on equal terms with England's most distinguished men, including the leaders of the British Bar' (p. 26).

33. Cecil, *Brief to Counsel*, p. 43. The following amusing note occurs in Sweet and Maxwell's *Guide to the Legal Profession*, 6th edn (London: Sweet and Maxwell, 1963) p. 15:

> Sir Harold Morris, QC, writing in 1930, said: 'The giving of a red bag is attended with a certain amount of ceremony. The King's Counsel hands it to his senior clerk and asks him kindly to convey it to Mr. So-and-So with his compliments. The senior clerk then hands it to the junior clerk who takes it round to the junior counsel's chambers and makes a formal presentation of the bag to him on the King's Counsel's behalf. It is the custom for the junior counsel then to hand a guinea to the junior clerk, who takes it back to the senior clerk and the latter pockets the sovereign and gives the shilling to the junior clerk for his work in the transaction.' *The Barrister.*

The custom is different in Canada, where a junior counsel has a blue bag, a Queen's Counsel a red bag, and a judge a green bag.

34. W. W. Boulton, *A Guide to Conduct and Etiquette at the Bar of England and Wales*, 4th edn (London: Butterworths, 1965) p. 10.

35. Sir Malcolm Hilbery, *Duty and Art in Advocacy* (London: Stevens, 1946) pp. 8–9. American lawyers have difficulty with this point. F. Lyman Windolph, in 'Trollope and the Law' in *Reflections of the Law in Literature* (Philadelphia: University of Pennsylvania Press, 1956) says, 'I do not know what the law on this subject is in England, but in the United States the course followed by Mr Chaffanbrass would be regarded as correct – even meticulously correct . . .' (pp. 26–7), and Clement Franklin Robinson, in 'Trollope's Jury Trials', *Nineteenth-Century Fiction*, 6 (December, 1952) p. 266, is similarly at a loss, saying, 'There is nothing sacred about a witness, although lawyers sometimes seem to think so.' American practice is no guide here.

36. Dickens, *The Posthumous Papers of the Pickwick Club*, New Oxford Illustrated Dickens (London: Oxford University Press, 1948) ch. XXXI, p. 427.

37. Hastings's views are very close to those of Chaffanbrass. 'I have always', says Hastings, 'made an inflexible rule never to see an accused person in his prison, lest I should find myself hampered in the conduct of the

defence, either by something the defendant may have said or by something he may have thought his counsel may have wished that he would say.' As for sympathy: 'It is no part of an advocate's duty to feel sympathy for his client, indeed any such feeling is rather a disadvantage than otherwise. The proper conduct of a defence in a grave and difficult case requires a cold-blooded detachment from any outside influence.' (Sir Patrick Hastings, *The Autobiography of Sir Patrick Hastings*. London: Heinemann, 1948, pp. 154 and 179). However, as Cecil says (in *Brief to Counsel*, p. 144), 'this is quite exceptional'.

38. The General Council of the Bar gave an opinion on what to do in such cases in 1915, advising that, if the confession came before the trial, counsel should refuse the case, since his heart would not be in it, and advise the client to seek other counsel. If the confession occurred during the trial, counsel might continue but neither suggest his client was innocent nor throw suspicion on anyone else known to be innocent. For a discussion of the issue with a vivid example see Carlton Kemp Allen, DCL, '*R. v. Dean*', *Law Quarterly Review*, 57 (1941) pp. 85–111.

39. Ballantine recalls the case in *Some Experiences of a Barrister's Life*, ch. VII.

40. Brian Abel-Smith and Robert Stevens, *Lawyers and the Courts: A Sociological Study of the English Legal System 1750–1965* (Cambridge, Mass.: Harvard University Press, 1967) p. 32.

41. Four professionals (apart from reviewers) examine in varying degrees of severity Trollope's technical competence in creating trials: Sir Francis Newbolt, '*Reg. v. Mason*', *Nineteenth Century*, 95 (1924), pp. 227–36; Henry S. Drinker, 'The Lawyers of Anthony Trollope', in *Two Addresses Delivered to Members of the Grolier Club*, 1950 (cited above); Clement Franklin Robinson, 'Trollope's Jury Trials', *Nineteenth-Century Fiction*, 1952 (cited above); and F. Lyman Windolph, *Reflections of the Law in Literature*, 1956 (cited above). Newbolt finds many faults in the *Orley Farm* trial but writes amusingly; Windolph's account of the *Phineas Redux* trial is largely synopsis.

4   *LARES ET PENATES*: SOLICITORS AND ESTATES

1. Harry Kirk, *Portrait of a Profession: A History of the Solicitor's Profession, 1100 to the Present Day* (London: Oyez Publishing, 1976) p. 16.
2. Charles Dickens, *The Old Curiosity Shop* (London: Oxford University Press New Oxford Illustrated Dickens, 1951) p. 98. Samuel Warren, *Moral, Social and Professional Duties of Attornies and Solicitors*, 1848, p. 347. See ch. 2, n. 4.
3. A. H. Manchester, *A Modern Legal History of England and Wales 1750–1850* (London: Butterworths, 1980) p. 54.
4. Kirk, p. 169.
5. James Boswell, *Life of Johnson*, ed. G. B. Hill and L. F. Powell, 6 vols (Oxford: Clarendon Press, 1934) vol. II, p. 126.
6. Kirk, pp. 169–71.

7. Slow and Bideawhile appear in *Doctor Thorne, Framley Parsonage, Orley Farm, Miss Mackenzie, He Knew He Was Right*, and *The Way We Live Now*.
8. Michael Birks, *Gentlemen of the Law* (London: Sweet and Maxwell, 1960) p. 246.
9. Charles Dickens, *The Battle of Life* in *Christmas Books*, New Oxford Illustrated Dickens (London: Oxford University Press, 1954) p. 251.
10. Sir Robert Megarry, *A Second Miscellany-at-Law* (London: Stevens, 1973) p. 48.
11. Sir Frederick Pollock, *The Land Laws* (London: Macmillan, 1896) pp. 119–20.
12. See Juliet McMaster's discussion of 'Trollope's Country Estates', in *Trollope Centenary Essays* (London: Macmillan, 1982) especially pp. 78–80.
13. Edmund Burke, *Reflections on the French Revolution* (London: Dent Everyman edition, 1910) pp. 31, 49 and 93–4.
14. Charles George Merewether (1823–84), educated at Wadham College, Oxford, became a barrister in 1848 and a QC in 1877. He was Recorder of Leicester from 1868. He stood for election at Northampton in 1868, 1874 and 1880 and was elected MP from 1874 to 1880. He was appointed in 1880 to a commission to inquire into corrupt election practices at elections. Though he wrote 'Turtle' Dove's opinion, there seems little else to connect him with Dove, whose fear of being beaten keeps him from Parliament. The *Northampton Radical* (October, 1874, p. 3) characterises Merewether as a 'thoroughly true blue church and State Tory, of the no progress kind' but possessed of 'charming *bonhomie* and frankness', whereas Dove is socially secretive and devoted to his books. Even appearing in court is distasteful to Dove. Trollope mentions Merewether's opinion on heirlooms in *An Autobiography*, Michael Sadleir and Frederick Page (eds), introduction by P. D. Edwards, (Oxford: Oxford University Press World's Classics Paperback, 1980) p. 116.
15. William Blackstone, *Commentaries on the Laws of England*, 4 vols (Oxford: 1745–49) vol. II, pp. 435–6.
16. Burke, *Reflections on the French Revolution*, p. 93.

5 THE LAW AND POLITICS

1. J. R. Vincent, *The Formation of the British Liberal Party, 1857–1868*, 2nd edn (Hassocks: Harvester Press, 1976) p. 39.
2. Ruth apRoberts, *Trollope: Artist and Moralist* (London: Chatto & Windus, 1971) p. 57.
3. Sir John Fortescue, *De Laudibus Legum Angliae*, ch. XLIX, quoted in John Matthews Manly, *Some New Light on Chaucer* (New York: Holt, 1926) p. 16.
4. Manly, 'Chaucer's Education', in *Some New Light on Chaucer*, pp. 29 and 44.
5. Daniel Duman, *The English and Colonial Bars in the Nineteenth Century* (London: Croom Helm, 1983) pp. 194–5.

166 *Trollope and the Law*

6. Ibid., p. 184. For example, appointments to judgeships.
7. Ibid.
8. Ibid., p. 187.
9. *Cobbett's Weekly Register*, Oct. 1806, quoted in Asa Briggs, *The Age of Improvement* (London: Longman, 1959) p. 105.
10. E. L. Woodward, *The Age of Reform, 1815–1870* (Oxford: Clarendon Press, 1938) p. 85 n. 4.
11. Briggs, *The Age of Improvement*, p. 266. Briggs is quoting Samuel Warren's *Manual of Election Law*, 1852.
12. William Ballantine, *Some Experiences of a Barrister's Life*, 2 vols (London: Bentley, 1882) vol. II, pp. 48–9.
13. See 'Part II: Parliament', in G. M. Young and W. D. Handcock (eds) *English Historical Documents*, vol. XII, 1833–1874 (London: Eyre & Spottiswoode, 1956).
14. *Statutes of the Realm*, 17 & 18 Vict., c. 102. (*English Historical Documents*, XII (I), pp. 145–8).
15. *Statutes*, 31 & 32 Vict., c. 125. (*English Historical Documents*, XII (I), pp. 184–6).
16. Ballantine, II, p. 41.
17. The connection between Trollope's personal experience of that election and the elections in *Ralph the Heir* and *Phineas Redux* is described in detail by John Halperin in his *Trollope and Politics: A Study of the Pallisers and Others* (London: Macmillan, 1977). In looking at some of the same material, I point out the legal content and bearings of these works.
18. James reported: 'I told them that if any person spent a farthing on my behalf he should never have it again from me, that I would rather lose the borough than spend a farthing. I also stated that I would make it a rule, if my supporters would allow me, however much it might interfere with my success, never to go to public houses for any votes other than the landlord's.' Quoted in Lord George R. Askwith, *Lord James of Hereford* (London: Benn, 1930) p. 18.
19. *Northampton Radical*, 9 Oct. 1874, p. 3.
20. *English Historical Documents*, vol. XII (I), 1833–1874, p. 114.
21. *Ibid.*, 'Report of commissioners on bribery at Sudbury in 1841', p. 136 (from *Parliamentary Papers*, 1844, XVIII).
22. Ibid., p. 137.
23. Ibid., p. 139.
24. Ibid., p. 136.
25. A similar bargain was revealed in the petition trial at Taunton, where Sir Henry James gained the seat from Serjeant Cox. It was shown that Cox, as a Conservative at the previous election, agreed to drop a petition if the Liberals neither at the next General Election nor in any earlier vacancy introduced a second Liberal candidate for Taunton, provided a second Conservative was not introduced. (Askwith, *Lord James of Hereford*, p. 19.)
26. Young and Handcock (eds) *English Historical Documents*, vol. XII (I), 1833–74, p. 113.
27. John Halperin, *Trollope and Politics: A Study of the Pallisers and Others*, p. 195.

28. Ballantine, II, pp. 43–5.
29. *Report of the Commissioners Appointed to Inquire into the Existence of Corrupt Practices at the Last Election and at Previous Elections of Members to sit in Parliament for the Borough of Beverley* (British Sessional Papers, House of Commons, 1870, vol. XXIX) p. 3.
30. *Ibid.*, VII, paragraph 8.
31. J. Edwards, *The Law Officers of the Crown* (London: Sweet and Maxwell, 1964) p. 5. Ambiguities also existed between the Law Officers' roles as prosecutors and as instruments of party policy. The office of Director of Public Prosecutions, under the supervision of the Attorney-General, was created in 1879 and united in 1884 with the office of Solicitor to the Treasury.
32. *Ibid.*, p. 5.
33. Thomas L. Shaffer, 'A Lesson from Trollope for Counselors at Law', *Washington and Lee Law Review*, 35 (1978) p. 727.
34. *Ibid.*, p. 732.
35. *Ibid.*, p. 743.
36. *Ibid.*, p. 733.
37. Halperin, *Trollope and Politics*, p. 274.
38. See Holdsworth, *A History of English Law*, vol. XV, pp. 405–15 and 429–37.
39. Duman, *The English and Colonial Bars in the Nineteenth Century*, p. 103, quoting Lord Cairns Papers, Public Record Office, MS 30/51/9 letter 47.

6 *LADY ANNA*: THE SOLICITOR-GENERAL AS PROSPERO

1. Blackstone, *Commentaries on the Laws of England*, 4 vols (Oxford: 1745–9) vol. I, 447.
2. The history of 'legitimate' theatre, of course, interestingly combines both senses of the word. Until 1843, legally a monopoly was held by Drury Lane, Covent Garden, and the Haymarket to produce five-act tragedy and comedy without music. Thus 'legitimate' theatre meant such performances as opposed to the 'burletta' with songs and music to which the minor theatres were technically restricted. The more general sense of legitimate theatre recorded by the OED: 'the body of plays, Shakespearian or other, that have a recognized theatrical or literary merit', stems from the supposedly higher status of the plays that would have been performed at the legitimate theatres.
3. P. D. Edwards, *Anthony Trollope, his Art and Scope*, (Hassocks: Harvester Press, 1978) p. 128.
4. MS Don. c. 10, vol. II, p. 7. That these notes precede the novel is evident from discrepancies between the two; for example, the notes show Trollope intended to have Lovel in a madhouse. The novel, however, is much more interesting in leaving the question of his madness less determinate, to be settled in court.

5. James Kincaid, *The Novels of Anthony Trollope*, (Oxford: Clarendon Press, 1977) p. 162.
6. *The Letters of Anthony Trollope*, N. John Hall (ed.) 2 vols (Stanford: Stanford University Press, 1983) p. 589.
7. Edwards, p. 129.
8. *Edinburgh Review*, XI, October 1807, p. 228, and XVII, February 1811, p. 434.
9. Shirley Letwin notes the care with which Trollope steers between conservative and radical class views here in *The Gentleman in Trollope: Individuality and Moral Conduct* (London: Macmillan, 1982) p. 124.
10. Edwards, p. 132.
11. Northrop Frye, *The Anatomy of Criticism* (Princeton: Princeton University Press, 1957) p. 174.
12. James, 'Anthony Trollope', in *Partial Portraits*, (London: Macmillan, 1888; reprinted Westport: Greenwood, 1970) pp. 100–1.
13. Frye, p. 163.
14. Frye, pp. 169–70.
15. Edmund Burke, *Reflections on the French Revolution*, (London: Dent Everyman, 1910), pp. 19–20.
16. Drinker, 'The Lawyers of Anthony Trollope', in *Two Addresses Delivered to Members of the Grolier Club* (New York: Grolier Club, 1950) p. 41.
17. The Supreme Court of Judicature had five divisions according to the Judicature Act of 1873–5. In addition to those named above, were the Court of Probate, Divorce and Admiralty, and the Court of Chancery. In 1880, the Courts of Queen's Bench, Common Pleas, and Exchequer were merged.
18. Burke, *Reflections on the French Revolution*, p. 153.

7 *MR. SCARBOROUGH'S FAMILY*: THE IDEA OF THE LAW

1. William Blackstone, *Commentaries on the Laws of England*, 4 vols (Oxford: 1745–9), I, pp. 39–41. It is true that later Blackstone inconsistently sets out the doctrine of Parliamentary law, arguing that 'parliament is always of absolute authority . . . if the parliament will positively enact a thing to be done which is unreasonable, I know of no power in the ordinary forms of the constitution, that is vested with authority to control it' (I, pp. 90–1).
2. George Sabine, *A History of Political Theory*, 3rd edn (London: Harrap, 1951) p. 509. S. M. Waddams notes:

   Though an early English court once suggested that Parliament itself could not validly legislate contrary to the law of God, and in 1614 a court said 'Even an Act of Parliament made against natural equity, as to make a man judge in his own case, is void in itself' [*Day* v. *Savadge* (1614) Hob. 85 at 87], it has long been the settled view in England that Parliament is absolutely supreme and can enact any law it wishes. The courts are interpreters only, and cannot override the parliamentary will. In the United States, on the other hand, the idea of the supremacy of the law of God or (in its secular form) natural law, took a strong hold, (*Introduction to the Study of Law* [Toronto: Carswell, 1979], p. 137.)

3. Jeremy Bentham, *A Comment on the Commentaries and a Fragment on Government*, J. H. Burns and H. L. A. Hart (eds) (London: The Athlone Press, 1977), pp. 10, 13, 58–9. Bentham's *A Comment on the Commentaries* was not published until 1928.
4. Blackstone, vol. I, 44.
5. Bentham, pp. 53–4.
6. Hume, *A Treatise on Human Nature*, L. A. Selby-Bigge (ed.) (Oxford: Clarendon Press, 1888) Book III, Part I, Section 1, p. 469.
7. Michael Timko, 'The Victorianism of Victorian Literature', *New Literary History*, 6 (1975), pp. 607–27. See also Walter M. Kendrick, *The Novel-Machine: The Theory and Fiction of Anthony Trollope* (Baltimore and London: Johns Hopkins, 1980) ch. 7.
8. Ernest Barker, *Principles of Social and Political Theory*, (Oxford: Clarendon Press, 1951) pp. 117–18.
9. Edmund Spenser, *The Faerie Queene*, Book I, Canto IX, stanza 53.
10. In C. G. Jung's view, Yahweh himself has his comic side. See Jung's *Answer to Job*, trans R. F. C. Hull (London: Routledge, 1954).
11. Bradford A. Booth, *Anthony Trollope: Aspects of his Life and Work* (London: Hulton, 1958) p. 130. James R. Kincaid, in *The Novels of Anthony Trollope* (Oxford: Clarendon Press, 1977), sees Scarborough as 'A kind of moral-philosophical Robin Hood' with ' a special sort of *duty* quite distinct from the old aristocratic notions of responsibility' (p. 253). A. O. J. Cockshut says, 'he hates entails, not simply because they interfere with his plans, but with the abiding metaphysical hatred of the political theorist' – see his *Anthony Trollope* (London: Collins, 1955) p. 231. Booth echoes Michael Sadleir's comment that *'Mr Scarborough's Family* is a novel of property' (*Trollope: A Commentary*, new edn rev. [London: Constable, 1945] p. 192.
12. Blackstone, vol. II, 2.
13. See Juliet McMaster, *Trollope's Palliser Novels: Theme and Pattern* (London: Macmillan, 1978) pp. 99–101.
14. Cockshut, p. 233.
15. Blackstone's language, *Commentaries*, vol. II, 16.
16. On Jane Austen's reverence for trees as a sign of sound character and social values, see Alistair M. Duckworth, *The Improvement of the Estate* (Baltimore: Johns Hopkins, 1971) pp. 53–4.
17. J. Edward Christian's note to his edition of Blackstone (London: 1809), vol. III, p. 223, n. 1.
18. Blackstone, vol. III, p. 228.
19. William Makepeace Thackeray, *Barry Lyndon* in George Saintsbury (ed.) *The Oxford Thackeray*, 17 vols, (London: Oxford University Press, 1908) vol. VI, pp. 240–1.
20. Blackstone, vol. III, pp. 225–6.
21. Christian's note, Blackstone, vol. II, p. 283, n. 13.

22. My colleague, Professor W. F. Bowker, QC draws my attention to the fact that the same rule about equitable waste is still preserved in the Alberta Judicature Act (Section 34 [(3)]) which specifies: 'An estate for life without any impeachment of waste does not confer and shall not be deemed to have conferred upon the tenant for life a legal right to commit waste of the description known as equitable waste, unless an intention to confer the right expressly appears by the instrument creating the estate.'

23. Christian's note, Blackstone vol. II, p. 283, n. 13. The original case report (2 *Vern.* 738) comes even closer to Scarborough: 'The Defendant the Lord *Barnard* having taken some Displeasure against his Son, got two *Hundred* Workmen together, and of a sudden, in a few Days, stript the Castle of the Lead, Iron, Glass Doors, and Boards, etc. to the value of 3000 L.'

24. James Kincaid says: 'they love one another . . . with a warmth particularly inexplicable to Grey. Each cannot but recognize instinctively the basic decency of the other, even though they are driven so far apart by the incoherence of things as they are.' *The Novels of Anthony Trollope*, p. 255.

25. Booth, p. 131.

26. Kincaid, p. 256.

27. For an account of the disaster, see Michael Sadleir, *Trollope, A Commentary*, ch. 2.

28. Sir Edward Coke, *Institutes*, I, 36 b, quoted in Blackstone, vol. II, p. 137.

29. Blackstone, vol. II, p. 136.

30. Robert M. Polhemus, in *The Changing World of Anthony Trollope* (Berkeley and Los Angeles: University of California Press, 1968) p. 241, sees the tension between Grey and Scarborough as a mellow accommodation of two social urges in the late Trollope: 'the urge to live by a communal moral code and an opposite urge to defy public opinion and make his own rules . . . the cultural ideal of the Victorians – an ideal which Trollope accepted and helped shape – was individual freedom in a moral society. They needed both Grey and Scarborough.'

Index

The entry for Trollope has been reserved for references to his life, experience of law, and attitudes towards it. Discussions of his novels, and of characters in them that receive more than passing mention, are indexed separately under titles and names. Reference to works by other writers are indexed under the writer's names. Italicised page numbers indicate sustained discussion. The following abbreviations are employed:

AA	An Autobiography	MM	Miss Mackenzie
AS	The American Senator	MSF	Mr./Scarborough's Family
BE	The Belton Estate	NZ	The New Zealander
CYFH	Can You Forgive Her	OF	Orley Farm
DC	The Duke's Children	PF	Phineas Finn
ED	The Eustace Diamonds	PM	The Prime Minister
HKHWR	He Knew He Was Right	PR	Phineas Redux
IHP	Is He Popenjoy?	RH	Ralph the Heir
LA	Lady Anna	TC	The Three Clerks
LC	The Life of Cicero	TW	The Warden
MB	The Macdermots of Ballycloran	WWLN	The Way We Live Now

Abel-Smith, Brian, and Stevens, 159

advocacy,
  ethics of, 6–11; Ben Jonson on, 7; Jonathan Swift on, 7–8; Thomas Macauley on, 8; Samuel Johnson on, 8; Thomas Erskine on, 9; Sir James Fitzjames Stephen on, 9;

Aeschylus
  Oresteia, 30
Alderson, Sir Edward Hall, 56
Allen, C. K., 164
Allwinde, Mr (MB, NZ), 6, 22, 55, 60
Altick, Richard D., 157
Amedroz, Clara (BE), 13
American Senator, The, 16, 84
An Autobiography, 2, 43, 51, 149
  achievement of pathos in Lady Mason, 43

satisfaction with Chaffanbrass, 51
  the Beverley election, 99, 100, 103
  on Lady Anna, 120–1, 126
  father disappointed of inheritance, 149
Annesley, Harry (MSF), 135, 148–9
apRoberts, Ruth, 90, 158
Archbold, John Frederick
  A Digest of the Law Relative to Pleading and Evidence in Actions Real Personal and Mixed, 4
Aristotle, 7
Arnold, Matthew, 133
Armstrong, Isobel
  'Browning and Victorian Poetry of Sexual Love', 44, 48
Athenaeum, 10, 133
Austen, Jane, 12, 169

171

estates, 12–18
mystique of, 74–6, 85
etiquette
of consultation with lay clients,
29, *32–49*; Brougham on,
34–5; Lord Chief Justice
Campbell on, 35; Serjeant
Pulling on, 35
of interviewing opposition
witnesses, 63–4, 163
concerning client's guilt or
innocence, 65
of conferences between
barristers and solicitors,
159–60
what to do if client confesses,
164
Eustace Diamonds, 10, 21, *76–84*,
91, 99, 121
heirlooms in, 79–81; difference
from *paraphernalia*, 80–1
Eustace, Lizzie (*ED*), 21, 30, 67,
76–84, 141
Exodus, 40

Fawn, Frederick, Viscount (*PR,
ED*), 50, 55, 63, 64, 66, 67, 77
attitude to his solicitor, 78
fine (*finalis concordia*), 13
Finn, Phineas (*PF, PR, PM, DC*),
63
demands belief in innocence as
well as acquittal, 64–6
a paper barrister 90, 96–7
Tankerville election, 66, 99
Forsyth, William, 92–3, 162
receives Brougham's elaboration
on duty to client, 162
Hortensius, 92
History of Trial by Jury, 93
Life of Cicero, 93
*Novels and Novelists of the
Eighteenth Century*, 93
Fortescue, Sir John, LCJ, 95
Framley Parsonage, 10
Freeling, Sir Francis, 4
Frye, Northrop, 128
Furnival, Thomas (*OF*), *32–49*,
145

desire affecting judgement,
38–9
and opinion of client's guilt, 40,
160

Gaskell, Elizabeth, 11
Garrick Club, 10, 133
Germain, Lord George (*IHP*), 26–7
Gladstone, William Ewart, 96
says offices of Attorney-General
and Solicitor-General no
guarantee of judgeships,
116
Goesler, Madame Max (*PF, PR,
ED, PM, DC*), 66
Gotobed, Senator (*AS*), 16
Graham, Felix (*OF*), 59
Grantly, Bishop (*TW*), 112
Grantly, Rev. Theophilus,
Archdeacon (*TW*), 110, 112–4
Grey, Dolly (*MSF*), 136, *147–8*
Grey, John (*MSF*), 6, 135, *145–8*
and the sanctity of law, 136, 139
one of Trollope's most attractive
lawyers, 145–8
Grey and Barry (*MSF*), 70, 71,
135, 146–7, 151–2
Grimm, Jacob and Wilhelm
'The Valient Little Tailor', 131
Grogram, Sir Gregory (*PR, PM*),
63
on bribery, at petition trial,
104–5
as Attorney-General, 114–17
Grotius, Hugo, 136

Hall, N. John, 168
Halperin, John, 105, 114, 155,
158, 166
Haphazard, Sir Abraham (*TW*),
109–14, 145
Harding, Septimus (*TW*), 109–14
Hastings, Sir Patrick, 65
on cold-blooded detachment
from client, 164
Hawkins, Henry, Baron
Brampton, 52, 54
*Reminiscences of Sir Henry
Hawkins*, 52, 161